Dice Works
for kids
math games
using special dice
box cars
and
one-eyed jacks®
Volume III

6th Printing – July 2007

1992 Written by: Joanne Currah, Jane Felling, Cheryl MacDonald

"Box Cars" won the National Learning Disabilities Association Idea of the Year 1991.

Revised Edition 1996, games written by: Joanne Currah, Jane Felling

ISBN: 0-9681613-7-5

ACKNOWLEDGEMENT

To our families -

for their continued support,
help and encouragement to

"Go for it!"

Jane & Joanne

The Fellings

John
Chris &
Andrea

The Currahs

Cameron
Richelle
Connor
Mackenzie &
Madison

TABLE OF CONTENTS

Multiplication and Division

Mixed Operations

INTRODUCTION

Why a revised edition for **Math Games with Special Dice** Box Cars and One-Eyed Jacks Volume III? The simple answer is that we have learned so much more about the special 10, 12 and 20-sided dice and the potential for teaching and exploring math concepts since we started playing with them in 1992.

The game activities that we first created have changed and developed through our continuing work with students at the classroom level. As a result we've had many opportunities to develop and create new games based on what we observed students doing with the materials.

We've felt for a long time that our "First Edition" just scratched the surface of what could be done with the special dice. So as a reprint deadline approached we decided to publish the games we've collected and developed over the years with the original ones. We know this book can now stand alone and be a worthy member of our Box Cars series of games books.

Math Games with Special Dice, Revised Edition contains 31 new games for a total of 80 games. We've tried to select a balance of games for K - 7. We've also added suggested grade levels to all games and now have an appendix of skills for easy reference.

We hope you enjoy our newest games and especially the endlessly fascinating dice that go with them.

Have Fun!

Joanne & Jane

HOW TO USE THIS BOOK

MATH GAMES WITH SPECIAL DICE, Vol. III, (revised edition 1996) contains 80 games and is divided into 5 sections:

1. Nuts and Bolts - Place Value Games
2. Addition and Subtraction
3. Multiplication and Division
4. Mixed Operations
5. Odds and Ends

Within each section the games are organized using the following format:

LEVEL:	appropriate grade level, intended to be flexible.
SKILLS:	specific math skills and pre-requisite skills are listed.
PLAYERS:	number needed for playing - intended to be flexible. You may change rules to add or subtract players, or adapt to solitaire.
EQUIPMENT:	specific items are listed, including which card values are needed. Counters should always be made available. Cards, dice, paper, pencil and counters are all that is needed to play any of the games.
GETTING STARTED:	rules and instructions which can be changed to meet individual needs.
VARIATIONS:	ideas to increase or decrease difficulty or to change/ add a skill.

The games do not have to be played in a set order. Teachers and parents can select games to:

1. introduce a concept or skill
2. practice a concept or skill
3. master a concept or skill

The games grew out of meeting the needs of our students. The first games we ever used were traditional WARS and SNAPS. The games proved so successful in helping our students, that we began to manipulate the rules of these games to work on other skills. You will find endless variations of these two traditional games.

Traditional War Type Games

War Type Games are for repetition and practice when a skill or concept is first introduced. Repeated exposure and repetition is the goal. War type games are excellent for players of different skill levels to play together to allow for peer teaching and support. Children are always encouraged to verbalize their answers and to share strategies with each other. Teachers may wish to change the term "war" to one of their own personal choice.

Traditional Snap Type Games

Snap Games are found throughout the book. These games are intended for use once a skill has been taught, understood and internalized by the child. Mastery of skills and concepts is the goal. Children of the same ability level should play together.

Snaps are an excellent way to start your math class. We nicknamed them "Manipulative Mad Minutes" and use them regularly in our program as a Math Warm-Up for our students. Playing for 2-5 minutes a day is time well spent. Many times the students did not play competitively. They simply played for the practice and fun of it!

The rules and instructions for all games are meant to be flexible. We encourage you to change the equipment, skills and rules, such as how to determine the winner. As you play more of the games you will discover how easy it is to change them. You will invent a new game in the process. Many of the games in our book were created in just this way.

Many of the games rely on luck to determine the eventual winner of the game. This is usually done by the throw of a regular die. Children will learn that winning is not always the most important aspect of the game. Many times the children played the games just for the practice and the fun of it, and there was no winner at all. We make it a point to have our students verbalize their math as they play. They verbalize their answers, their math sentences, strategies, etc. This repetitive practice is central to each and every game. It is the key element that makes these games practical for use in the school and home.

Materials

All games incorporate the use of special multi-sided dice; either 10, 12, or 20-sided. Some games may require the use of the following additional materials:

playing cards, bingo chips or other suitable counters,
reproducible gameboards, paper, pencil, calculators.

So what are the dice ideal for?

10-Sided Dice

This die is numbered 0, 1, 2, 3, 4, 5, 6, 7, 8, 9, (6 and 9 are underlined for reference), and is ideal for exploring the following concepts:

PRIMARY K - 3

- Recognizing numbers to 9
- Rolling two or more dice and building two-digit place value numbers such as 6 3 sixty-three or 9 8 2 nine-hundred eighty-two, etc.
- Rolling two dice and adding to 18, eg. 6 + 8 = 14

- Working with doubles - rolling a die and doubling its value (see We Love Doubles, p. 38) eg. 8 doubled = 8 + 8 = 16
- Rolling two dice and subtracting eg. 9 - 2 = 7
- Graphing
- Probability experiments
- Exploring patterns

INTERMEDIATE 4 - 7

- All of the above plus:
- Rolling two dice and multiplying products to 81
- Problem solving with multi-operational activities

12-Sided Dice

This die is numbered 1, 2, 3, 4, 5, 6, 7, 8, 9, 10, 11, 12 (6 and 9 are underlined for reference), and is ideal for exploring the following concepts:

PRIMARY K - 3

- Time on the clock
- Months of the year
- Fractions
- Recognizing numbers to 12
- Rolling two dice and adding facts to 24 (may involve regrouping)
- Rolling two dice and subtracting facts from 12
- Working with the doubles
- Graphing
- Probability experiments
- Exploring patterns

INTERMEDIATE 4 - 7

- All of the above plus:
- Rolling two dice and multiplying products to 144
- Problem solving / multi-operational activities

20-Sided Dice

This die is numbered 1, 2, 3, 4, 5, 6., 7, 8, 9., 10, 11, 12, 13, 14, 15, 16., 17, 18, 19, 20. (6., 9., 16., and 19. have a dot for reference), and is ideal for exploring the following concepts:

PRIMARY K - 3

- Recognizing numbers to 20 especially the "teens"
- Rolling two dice and adding facts to 40 (may involve regrouping and 2-digit to 2-digit addition)
- Rolling two dice and subtracting facts from 20 (may involve 2-digit from 2-digit)
- Working with the doubles
- Graphing
- Probability experiments
- Exploring patterns

INTERMEDIATE 4 - 7

- All of the above plus:
- Estimating and mental math activities
- Problem solving / multi-operational activities
- Place value building numbers to 2020

Special dice are hard to resist and may go missing. So for consistency we count out and collect the dice before and after each games period. The dice need to be rolled on a flat, level surface. Children will quickly learn to read the top number, and recognize the visual cues for 6 and 9 (we tell them the line is a printing line) and the 6., 9., 16., and 19. Children usually use the dice with a partner. However the dice are so popular that many classrooms hold a fundraiser, such as a popcorn or bake sale to purchase entire class sets.

Organization

Games were a part of every lesson. We allowed anywhere from ten to twenty minutes for math games every day. As well, children could play math games during free time/center time. It is important that play and practice time be consistent for all students. The games were not used as rewards and all students played. Usually students were given a choice of games and selected one that was the most appropriate. Pairs and groups were selected initially by the teacher. This ensures appropriate groupings. Pairings and groupings were changed frequently.

The games were usually taught to the entire group first. The class usually played the game for a number of days until it was well understood. After a number of games had been taught on a single concept, the students or teacher would choose the one that was most appropriate for them to play. During a typical games period many different games can be played.

Teachers may wish their students to have a permanent record of the games period. Some teachers have students record some of their work in a permanent place such as a BOX CARS BOOK. A listing of the games played, strategies used, and skills to work on may be recorded.

Encourage children to play the games at home for extra practice. We often included a game in our newsletters that went home to parents. During parent-teacher interviews, when parents ask what they can do to help their children at home, have some game instructions available. Games are also useful activities to leave for a substitute teacher.

Box Cars games should complement your existing math program, not replace it. It is in this spirit we hope that MATH GAMES with SPECIAL DICE will be helpful to teachers and parents in meeting the needs of their children.

Finally, HAVE FUN!

– Joanne and Jane

Dear Parents:

This year your child's math program will include a games component. Key concepts will be repeated and practiced through exciting and fun games. The use of manipulatives will be an important part of the program.

Therefore, we are asking families to look for any used cards and dice that could be donated for class use. Decks of cards do not have to be complete.

Your contribution to our class is greatly appreciated. Look forward to your child teaching you some of our math games soon!

Thank you for your assistance,

Yours truly,

Section I

Nuts & Bolts

Place Value Games

ROLLING ALONG

LEVEL: Kindergarten to Grade 1

SKILLS: Number recognition, number matching

PLAYERS: 2 - 4

EQUIPMENT: One 12-sided die, paper, pencil

GETTING STARTED: Each player makes a gameboard as follows: (see reproducibles)

1 2 3 4 5 6 7 8 9 10 11 12

X X X

The object is for each player to cross off all their numbers on their gameboard. Player one rolls the die and crosses off that same number on their gameboard. Player two then takes a turn. Players continue to alternate turns. If a player rolls a number that has already been crossed off, they earn a strike. Three strikes and a player is out and cannot continue rolling. The game ends when all players are out, or one player gets all of their numbers crossed off. If all players strike out, the player with the most numbers crossed off is the winner.

VARIATION I: Use a 20-sided die and have a gameboard 1-20.

VARIATION II: Players create their number lines using a deck of cards Ace - Queen (Ace = 1, Jack = 11, Queen = 12). Players roll the die and turn over that same number card. The game ends when one player turns over all of their cards.

NUMBO

LEVEL: Kindergarten to Grade 1

SKILLS: Number recognition to 20

PLAYERS: 4

EQUIPMENT: One 20-sided die, one 20-squared bingo gameboard per player (standard or random, see reproducibles), bingo chips

GETTING STARTED: Each player rolls once, the player with the lowest roll goes first. Each player has their own bingo card. Players alternate rolling the die and covering the appropriate number on their gameboard. The number rolled is used just for that player. The player who gets five in a row horizontally, vertically or diagonally first wins that round.

VARIATION I: For solitaire, the player places a "tick" for each roll and sees how many rolls it takes to get a NUMBO!

VARIATION II: Players agree that only a horizontal row is acceptable - or just vertical or diagonal.

COUNT 'EM AND EAT 'EM

LEVEL: Kindergarten to Grade 2

SKILLS: 1 to 1 correspondence of numbers to 12, counting to 100

PLAYERS: 2 or more

EQUIPMENT: One 12-sided die, bowl of cereal, "cube-a-links"

GETTING STARTED: Player one rolls the die and takes that number of "crunchies" from the bowl. Player two rolls the die and takes that number of crunchies. Players alternate turns until all players have had ten rolls. Players may need to keep track of how many rolls they have had. Each player could start with ten cubes linked together. At the beginning of each turn, the player breaks off one cube indicating they have one less turn to take. After each player has had ten turns, they may count up the total number of crunchies and eat them!

VARIATION: You could use a 20-sided die and have the students count up to twenty, limit to five rolls.

ROLL IT AND MARK IT

LEVEL: Kindergarten to Grade 2

SKILLS: Number recognition, writing numerals, graphing

PLAYERS: 2 - 4

EQUIPMENT: One 12-sided die, gameboard (see reproducibles)

GETTING STARTED: Each player has their own gameboard.

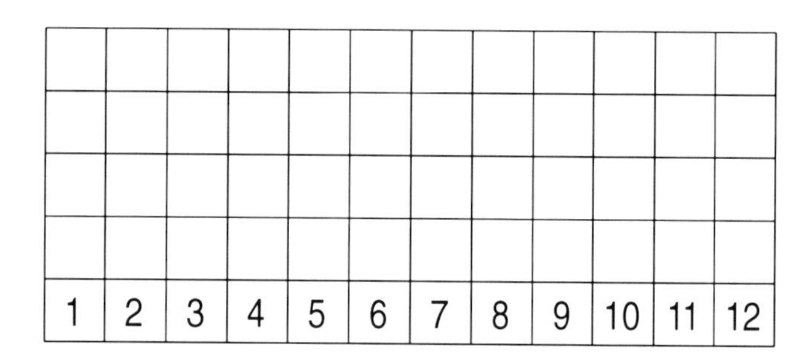

1	2	3	4	5	6	7	8	9	10	11	12

Player one rolls the die. Players must recognize the number on the die and write the corresponding numeral on their graph. Players alternate turns until one player has one horizontal row filled in. Encourage players to verbalize which number has been rolled the most, least, or same as another number.

EXAMPLE: A six is rolled, and the numeral six is recorded on their graph. If they roll another six it is also recorded etc.

					6						
					6			9			
1	2				6		8	9	10		
1	2	3	4	5	6	7	8	9	10	11	12

ODD AND EVEN

LEVEL: Grade 1 - 3

SKILLS: Number recognition, odd/even

PLAYERS: 2 - 4

EQUIPMENT: One 12-sided die, 100 "cube-a-links" (minimum); two colours – 50 of each (one colour to represent even numbers, and one colour to represent odd numbers)

GETTING STARTED: Player one rolls the die and determines whether the number is even or odd. If even, the player takes the appropriate number of even coloured cubes and links these together. If odd, they take the appropriate number of odd coloured cubes. Player two takes a turn. Players continue alternating turns each building two separate rows of cubes (one to represent an even row and one to represent an odd row). After ten rolls players compare their odd and even "trains". The longest trains score 1 point.

VARIATION: Have players build two trains of fifty (one with each colour). Players roll and subtract from their odd and even trains. The first player to shrink their trains scores 1 point.

RACE TO THE TOP

LEVEL: Grade 1 and up

SKILLS: Number recognition, odd / even, probability

PLAYERS: 1 - 4

EQUIPMENT: Five 20-sided dice, gameboard (see reproducibles), paper, pencil

GETTING STARTED: Player one's gameboard rolled and filled in is as follows:

EXAMPLE:

	ODD	EVEN
10	7	
9	3	16
8	15	10
7	17	18
6	7	18
5	5	10
4	3	20
3	11	12
2	15	16
1	17	6

Each player needs their own gameboard. Player one rolls the die, verbalizes the number rolled and states whether it is an even or an odd number. Player one then records the number in the appropriate space. Players alternate turns rolling the die and filling in their own graphs. The first player to fill in all ten spaces on the 'even' or 'odd' column of their graph wins.

TEACHING TIP: When there is uncertainty re: odd and even, cubes can provide a good visual. Have students count out the number of cubes indicated on the die and snap them into equal halves. If they can, the number is even; if they can't, the number is odd.

MR. WOLF IS UPSIDE DOWN!

LEVEL: Kindergarten to Grade 2

SKILLS: Number recognition, number sequencing 1 - 12

PLAYERS: Solitaire or cooperative pair

EQUIPMENT: One 12-sided die, cards Ace - Queen (A = 1, Jack = 11, Queen = 12)

GETTING STARTED: Each player builds their own clock with cards Ace - Queen. All cards, except the Ace, are placed face down as follows:

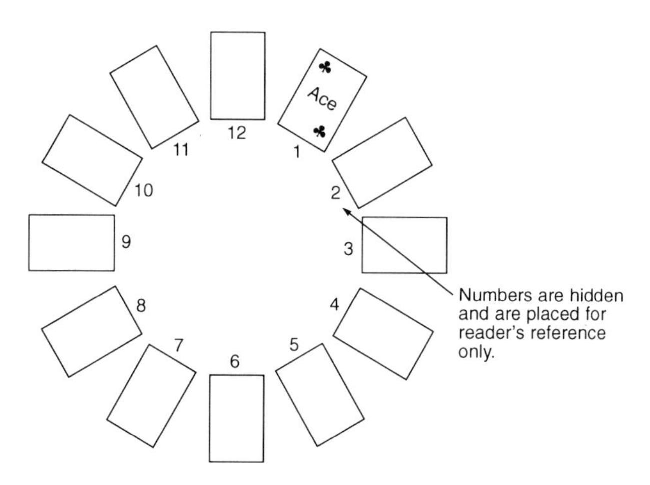

The goal of the game is to be the first player to turn over all their cards in their clock. Player one rolls the die and identifies the number rolled. The player must determine which hidden card matches the number rolled. Players do this by counting on from any visible number, counting back, or by learning the correct positions of the numbers on the clock face.

EXAMPLE: Player one rolls a 5 and would count on from Ace = 1, 2, 3, 4 and flip over number 5. Player two would take their turn. Player one rolls a 3. Player one could either count on from the Ace = 1, 2 and turn over the three or count back from the overturned 5… 4, 3.

Players continue to alternate rolling the die, identifying the number and turning over the corresponding card. If a player rolls a number already turned over, they miss that turn and their opponent proceeds.

The first player to turn over all cards on their clock is the winner.

TIME OUT

LEVEL: Kindergarten to Grade 2

SKILLS: Telling time to the hour

PLAYERS: 1 or more

EQUIPMENT: One 12-sided die, gameboard (see reproducibles)

GETTING STARTED: Each player draws a clock with the minute hand drawn in. Player one rolls the die and identifies the number rolled. This number becomes the hand the player may draw on their clock. Players take turns rolling and filling in the time on their own clock. The first player to complete their clock is the winner and calls "Time Out!"

VARIATION: Telling time to the half hour, quarter hour, and three-quarter hour may also be worked on by changing the position of the hands on the clock.

Roll two 12-sided dice and players may add or subtract them and cross out the time. (ie., roll 6 and 5 and you may cross out 11 o'clock or 1 o'clock). The first player to cross off all their numbers is the winner.

PICK AND FREEZE

LEVEL: Grade 1 - 3

SKILLS: Comparing numbers, greater than/less than, odd/even

PLAYERS: 2

EQUIPMENT: One 20-sided die per player, cards Ace - 9 (Ace = 1), (a 10 or 12-sided dice may be substituted)

GETTING STARTED: Each player rolls their die three times and chooses the best least, or best greatest number. These numbers are recorded and player circles the number selected. To determine which player earns the point for the round a card is then turned over.

ODD CARD: The player with the lowest/least number keeps the card.

EVEN CARD: The player with the highest/greatest number keeps the card.

EXAMPLE:

	Roll #1	Roll #2	Roll #3
Player One *chooses best greatest	(20)	4	8
Player Two *chooses best least	9	6	(3)

Play continues for a set period of time. The player with the most cards is the winner.

In the event of a tie (ie., both players choose the same number) both players may take a card for a point.

VARIATION: For Kindergarten use 10-sided die and have two rolls only.

BETWEEN FRIENDS

LEVEL: Kindergarten to Grade 2

SKILLS: Sequencing numbers 1 - 20

PLAYERS: 3

EQUIPMENT: One 20-sided die per player, bingo chips or other counters

GETTING STARTED: All players roll their die. Players compare their numbers by first arranging them in sequence and then determining which number falls in the middle. The middle or "between" number wins. A number line can also provide a good visual for younger students who are still learning to determine betweenness given three numbers.

EXAMPLE: Rolls - 1, 5, 18

[1] 2 3 4 [5] 6 7 8 9 10 11 12 13 14 15 16 17 [18] 19 20

Players place their die on the number line and determine 1 is least, 18 is greatest, and 5 falls in between.

Players should verbalize the relationship between the rolled numbers. The player who rolled 5 would take a chip (point) for the round.

There may be some rounds where no players earn a point (ie., roll 16, 12, 16).

1 2 3 4 5 6 7 8 9 10 11 [12] 13 14 15 [16] 17 18 19 20
[16]

There is no between number.

Players continue rolling, arranging the numbers and determining the between/middle number. Play continues for a set period of time. The player with the most points is the winner.

A DETECTIVE'S ROLL

LEVEL: Grade 1 - 3

SKILLS: Place value, odd and even numbers, betweenness

PLAYERS: Groups of 4-6

EQUIPMENT: One 20-sided die per player

GETTING STARTED: A "detective" is chosen for the group. The detective's job is to determine the value of each player's roll. Players secretly roll their die. The detective then gives the following instructions: "All players who rolled 10 or less sit down." This becomes the detective's first clue. The detective then selects a player for "questioning." The detective is allowed two questions per player. Examples: "Is your number odd or even?" or "Is your number between 15 and 20?". The detective must now guess that player's number. If correct, the detective scores one point. If not, the other player scores a point. The detective selects the next player and proceeds to guess their number. A new detective is selected after all players have been questioned. Play ends when all players have been the detective. The player with the most points wins.

VARIATION: Players roll two 10-sided dice and make a number between 0 and 99. The detective is now allowed four to eight questions per player in attempt to guess the value of their roll.

TEACHING TIP: It may be helpful to appoint a "secretary" to record the information gathered by the "detective". The continuous score may also be recorded.

SECRET ROLL

LEVEL: Grade 1 - 3

SKILLS: Probability, using logical reasoning, making predictions

PLAYERS: 2

EQUIPMENT: Two 20-sided dice

GETTING STARTED: The goal of the game is to have a correct prediction. Players score 1 point for each correct prediction.

TEACHING TIP: Teach the game to one pair of children at a time. Before explaining the rules, roll both dice in front of the players and have them identify the greatest roll and the least roll. Do this to provide enough practice to ensure they understand this concept before proceeding with the game.

STEP 1 - ROLLING THE DIE:

To begin each round each player secretly rolls their die. They must look at their number and decide whether it is most probably the greatest or least of the two hidden rolls. Players decide on their predictions.

STEP 2 - PREDICTIONS:

Note: As players gain experience with this game their predictions will become more accurate. An understanding of probability will only come with practice.

First Predictions: In sequence each player states their prediction. Important information can be gathered by players at this point and used for the second round of predictions.

Second Predictions: This is the last round for players to make predictions. Based on information from the first round, player may either stay with their original first round prediction or change it. Again in sequence, each player states one of the following:

1) I'm staying with greatest or least (their first round prediction).

2) I'm changing my prediction to greatest or least.

During this second round players must use logical reasoning and their understanding of probability to determine the best prediction for their own secret roll.

STEP 3 - REVEALING THE ROLLS:

Once the second round of predictions are completed, players reveal their secret rolls. Players compare their predictions to the actual ranking of their own roll. Players score a point if their prediction is correct.

Note: Players should rotate turns being the first to predict each new round.

SKIP AWAY

LEVEL: Grade 1 - 3

SKILLS: 1 to 1 correspondence of numbers, counting to 20, patterned counting for beginning multiplication

PLAYERS: 2 or more

EQUIPMENT: One 20-sided die, "cube-a-links", paper, pencil

GETTING STARTED: Player one rolls the die and takes that number of "cube-a-links" to link together. Players alternate rolling the die. Play continues until all players have had ten rolls. Players count up their cubes. The player with the most cubes is the winner. Players may need to keep track of how many rolls they have had. They may keep track tallying with paper and pencil. For multiplication, count each cube using 2's, 5's and 10's pattern or players may wish to count off 10's "trains" and use place value mats to determine their totals.

MATCH MAKERS

LEVEL: Kindergarten and up

SKILLS: Place value, number recognition

PLAYERS: 2 - 4

EQUIPMENT: Two 10-sided dice, cards Ace - 9 (Ace = 1), King (K = 0)

GETTING STARTED: Each player is dealt four cards. Player one rolls both dice and verbalizes their number in place value. The digits may be manipulated by the roller to make the number of their choice (ie., 4 and 7 = 47 or 74).

All players look in their hands in attempt to create this number using the cards as place value holders. If more than one combination can be laid, the player may lay down as many cards as possible.

EXAMPLE: **Player one** rolls a 5 and 2.

Player one's cards include:

2	King	3	6

Player two's cards include:

1	4	2	5

Player two lays down a

2	5

and verbalizes "twenty-five".

Player two now replenishes to four cards and player one keeps the same four cards. Player two then rolls a new number and play continues. The winner is the first player to lay down all four cards on one turn or whoever has laid down the most cards after a set period of time.

HUNDRED BOARD TIC TAC TOE

LEVEL: Grade 1 and up

SKILLS: Identification of place value 1 - 100

PLAYERS: 2

EQUIPMENT: Hundred Board (see reproducibles), two 10-sided dice, bingo chips (1 colour per player)

GETTING STARTED: Players select a colour of marker. The goal of the game is for players to get three bingo chips of their own colour in a row, either horizontally, vertically or diagonally. Player one rolls the dice and makes a two-digit number (ie., roll 4 and 7 and verbalizes "4 tens, 7 ones, : forty-seven", OR "7 tens, 4 ones, : seventy-four"). Player then covers the two corresponding spaces on the Hundred Board. Player two then takes their turn, rolling the dice and covering both of their numbers, remembering to verbalize the tens and ones place value to their opponent. Players continue to alternate turns trying to get TIC TAC TOE - THREE IN A ROW. When this happens the player removes their markers and counts 2 points for each marker (6 points for three in a row).

CAPTURING AN OPPONENT'S SPACE: If a player rolls a two-digit number that is occupied by their opponent then that player removes their opponent's marker and replaces it with one of their own. Each captured marker is worth 5 points.

ROLLING YOUR OWN SPACE: If a player rolls a one or two-digit number that they already occupy, they may roll again to get a new number.

Players continue to alternate turns for a set period of time. At the end of play, the player with the most points is the winner.

PLACE VALUE TOSS UP

LEVEL: Grade 1 - 3

SKILLS: Place value to 100

PLAYERS: 2

EQUIPMENT: Two 10-sided dice per player

GETTING STARTED: Each player rolls their two dice and makes the largest two-digit number possible and verbalizes it to their partner. The player with the largest number scores 2 points.

EXAMPLE:

Player One	**Player Two**
6, 2 = 62	4, 3 = 43

Player one receives 2 points.

In the event of a tie (both players have the same number), a tie breaker must be played. Each player rolls the dice again to get another number between 1 - 100. The first player to roll a number greater than the tie scores 4 points.

EXAMPLE:

Player One	**Player Two**
6, 3 = 63	6, 3 = 63

Tie "63"

Tie Breaker

3, 8 = 38	7, 6 = 76

Player two receives 4 points because they have the largest number and it is greater than 63. Play continues until one player scores 50 points.

EXPANDER

LEVEL: Grade 4 and up

SKILLS: Expanding numbers, adding to 10,000

PLAYERS: Small groups, or teacher vs. whole class

EQUIPMENT: One 20-sided die, pencil, paper

GETTING STARTED: The goal of the game is to create the largest number possible. The player(s) with the largest number score 1 point for that round. Groups can play to a set score (ie., 10 or 20 points) or for a set amount of time. Each player makes a grid as follows:

Thousands	Hundreds	Tens	Ones

A player from the group is selected to roll the 20-sided die for the round. The die is rolled and each player must record that number somewhere on their grid. Once all players have filled in this number, the die is rolled again. This number is also placed in the grid. Two more rolls are taken to fill the grid, for a total of four rolls.

EXAMPLE: The four rolls are 12, 9, 6, 18

Player One

Th	Hu	T	O
18	12	9	6

Player Two

Th	Hu	T	O
12	18	9	6

At the end of the four rolls, players total their rolls as follows:

Player One

```
  18000
   1200
     90
+     6
  19296
```

Player Two

```
  12000
   1800
     90
+     6
  13896
```

Player one scores 1 point for the round.

If two or more players create the largest number they all score 1 point. Play continues until a player reaches a certain number of points or for a set period of time. The player with the most points wins.

Note: The more students play this game, the better their strategy will become.

VARIATION I: Change grid to incorporate more place values:

Ten Thousands	Thousands	Hundreds	Tens	Ones

VARIATION II: Include decimals:

Ten Thousands	Thousands	Hundreds	Tens	Ones	Tenths	Hundredths
				•		

ROCK N' ROLL

LEVEL: Grade 4 and up

SKILLS: Creating a five-digit number

PLAYERS: 2 - 4

EQUIPMENT: Five 10-sided dice per player

GETTING STARTED: All players roll their dice at the same time. Players then begin arranging their dice to make the largest five-digit number possible. The first player to finish calls out "Rock N' Roll" and verbalizes their number to the other players. All other players must freeze their numbers in their current order, even if they are not finished arranging them.

If the first player done is also the player with the largest number of the group they score 10 points. If not, they earn 5 points and the player who does have the highest number of the group would also earn 5 points. All other players earn 0. The first player to reach 50 points is the winner.

Addition & Subtraction

PUZZLING PLUSES

LEVEL: Grade 2 and up

SKILLS: Adding sums to 40

PLAYERS: 2

EQUIPMENT: Two 20-sided dice per player, paper, pencil, (10 or 12-sided dice may be substituted)

GETTING STARTED: Each player rolls two dice and adds the numbers together. The player with the greatest sum receives 2 points.

EXAMPLE:

Player One	Player Two
4 + 9 = 13	7 + 9 = 16

Player two would win 2 points.

In the event of a tie (each player has the same sum), a tie breaker must be played. Each player rolls their dice again and finds the sum. The first player to roll a sum greater than the tie scores 4 points.

EXAMPLE:

Player One	Player Two
7 + 3 = 10	5 + 5 = 10

Tie "10"

Player One	Player Two
4 + 3 = 7	2 + 3 = 5

Neither sum higher than 10, roll again.

Player One	Player Two
10 + 5 = 15	6 + 5 = 11

Player one receives 4 points for breaking the tie with a sum greater than the original roll.

Play continues until one player scores 50 points.

WE LOVE DOUBLES SNAP

LEVEL: Grade 1 and up

SKILLS: Immediate recall of doubles facts, addition to 18

PLAYERS: 2 (equal skill level)

EQUIPMENT: One 10-sided die, bingo chips

TEACHING TIP: Learning the doubles helps students tremendously with difficult addition combinations. For example, if a student knows that 7 + 7 = 14, then we want them to realize that 7 + 8 is really just a double plus one more. (7 + 7) + 1 = 15. We use the following nicknames for the most difficult doubles to help with recall.

6 + 6 = 12	Farmer's Double (12 eggs) or Box Cars
7 + 7 = 14	Valentine's Double (February 14)
8 + 8 = 16	"Sweet 16" or Sweetheart Double
9 + 9 = 18	Adult or Grownup Double

When any double appears in written work we encourage students to circle it and connect it to the doubles work we've done. After doubles are mastered we work on all the double plus one combinations

Double	Double Plus One
5 + 5 = 10	5 + 6 = 11
6 + 6 = 12	6 + 7 = 13
7 + 7 = 14	7 + 8 = 15
8 + 8 = 16	8 + 9 = 17
9 + 9 = 18	9 + 10 = 19

Eventually students may learn to generalize the answers to: addition doubles are even answers, and the doubles plus one answers are odd.

GETTING STARTED: The die is rolled and players double it to find the sum (ie., if a 6 is rolled the correct answer is 12). The first player to say the correct answer outloud collects a bingo chip. In the case of a tie (ie., both players give the correct answer at the same time), both players take a chip.

Play continues for a set period of time. The player with the most points (chips) is the winner.

VARIATION: Double plus one snap (ie., 7 is rolled, players double 7 + 7 = 14 add one and give the answer 15).

DOUBLE TROUBLE

LEVEL: Grade 2 and up

SKILLS: Adding doubles

PLAYERS: 2

EQUIPMENT: Two 10-sided dice per player, paper, pencil

GETTING STARTED: Each player makes a gameboard as follows:

2 4 6 8 10 12 14 16 18

The goal of the game is to be the first player to cross all the numbers off their board. Players take turns rolling their dice in an attempt to roll doubles. If a double is rolled, the player finds the sum and crosses it off of their gameboard. Players each get three rolls per turn. The first player to cross off all of their numbers is the winner.

EXAMPLE:

4 + 4 = 8 8 is crossed off
7 + 7 = 14 14 is crossed off

FAIR GAME ADDITION

LEVEL: Grade 2 and up

SKILLS: Adding to 40

PLAYERS: 2

EQUIPMENT: Four 20-sided dice, 1 regular die

GETTING STARTED: Each player rolls two 20-sided dice and adds them together. Player one rolls the regular die to determine who wins the point:

1, 3, 5 (odd) roll – least sum wins the point.
2, 4, 6 (even) roll – greatest sum wins the point.

Players continue to roll the dice and add them together. Players alternate the roll of the regular die. If players roll equal sums, each player scores 1 point. The first player to score 20 points is the winner.

WINNING TRACK CHALLENGER

LEVEL: Grade 2 and up

SKILLS: Adding, subtracting, multiplying, and dividing number combinations to 12

PLAYERS: 1 - 4

EQUIPMENT: One 12-sided die, One 10-sided die, gameboard (see reproducibles), pencil, paper

GETTING STARTED: Each player draws a gameboard as follows:

0 1 2 3 4 5 6 7 8 9 10 11 12

X X X

Player number one rolls both dice. Players may cross off up to three open numbers that, when combined, total up to that roll. For example, 8 and 2 are rolled. Player may now cross off any combinations that equal ten: 8 + 2, 12 – 2, 2 x 5, 10 – 0, 0 + 4 + 6, (12 ÷ 3) + 6, 11 - 1 - 0, etc. Only one combination can be crossed off per turn. Player two may then take a turn. Players continue to alternate turns. If a player rolls a sum that is impossible to cross off any number or combination for, the player earns a strike, circling the X. Three strikes and a player is out and cannot continue rolling. The game ends when all players are out, or one player gets all numbers on their gameboard crossed off. If all players strike out, the player with the most numbers crossed off is the winner.

“Dear Joanne & Jane,

Thank you for coming to our school. I liked the dice, they were cool. And the game Winning Track Challenger was very fun. Do you like your books? My favourite dice were the green ones.”

yours truly,
B.F.
Grade four

ROLL AND FLIP

LEVEL: Grade 2 and up

SKILLS: 3 addend addition

PLAYERS: 2 - 4

EQUIPMENT: Two 10-sided dice per player, cards Ace - 6 (Ace = 1) (Grade 2 - 3); Ace - 10 (Ace = 1) (Grade 4 and up)

GETTING STARTED: Each player rolls their dice and flips over one card. Players add all the numbers and determine their sum. The player with the greatest sum takes their opponent's card. This is put to the side to be counted as points at the end of the game. In the event of a tie, (both players have the same sum) players flip up an additional new card and add this on to their previous sum. The player with the greatest grand sum earns all the cards. Play continues for a set period of time. The player with the most cards (points) collected is the winner.

EXAMPLE:

Player One card

Roll: 4, 6 + [3] = 13

Player Two card

Roll: 6, 8 + [8] = 22

Player two collects player one's card and places it with their own card in their point pile.

VARIATION: To increase the difficulty have players multiply their rolled numbers and add this product to the flipped up card for a total sum. Players then compare their sums. The player with the greatest sum collects the cards.

ADDITION TIC TAC TOE

LEVEL: Grade 2 and up

SKILLS: Addition facts to 18

PLAYERS: 2

EQUIPMENT: Two 10-sided dice, bingo chips (1 colour per player), addition table to 18 (see reproducibles)

GETTING STARTED: Players select a colour of markers. The goal of the game is for players to get three bingo chips of their own colour in a row, either horizontally, vertically or diagonally. Player one rolls the dice and adds them together, verbalizing the sum to their opponent (ie., player rolls 6 + 8; verbalizes "6 + 8 = 14 and 8 + 6 = 14") and covers the two corresponding spaces on the gameboard. Player two now rolls and covers their corresponding spaces on the gameboard. Players continue to alternate turns trying to get TIC TAC TOE - THREE IN A ROW. When this happens, the player removes their markers and counts 2 points for each marker (6 points for three in a row).

CAPTURING AN OPPONENT'S SPACE: If a player rolls a sum that is occupied by their opponent then that player removes their opponent's marker and replaces it with one of their own. Each captured marker is worth 5 points.

ROLLING YOUR OWN SPACE: If a player rolls a sum that they already occupy, they may roll again to get a new sum.

Players continue to alternate turns for a set period of time. At the end of play, the player with the most points is the winner.

ADDITION SNAP

LEVEL: Grade 2 and up

SKILLS: Immediate recall of addition facts to 24

PLAYERS: 2 (equal skill level)

EQUIPMENT: Two 12-sided dice

GETTING STARTED: At the same time, each player rolls one of the die. Players must add the two numbers together. The first player who says the correct sum outloud scores 1 point. In the event of a tie, no one scores a point. Play continues for a set period of time or until a certain number of points have been reached.

TRIPLE SNAP

LEVEL: Grade 3 and up

SKILLS: Immediate recall of three addends, adding to 30

PLAYERS: 3 (equal skill level)

EQUIPMENT: Three 10-sided dice

GETTING STARTED: At the same time, each player rolls one of the die. Players must add the three numbers rolled. The first player who says the correct sum outloud scores 1 point. In the event of a tie, no one scores a point. Play continues for a set period of time or until a certain number of points have been reached.

SNAP TO 40

LEVEL: Grade 3 and up

SKILLS: Immediate recall of addition facts to 40

PLAYERS: 2 (equal skill level)

EQUIPMENT: Two 20-sided dice

GETTING STARTED: At the same time, each player rolls one of the die. Players must add the two numbers together. The first player who says the correct sum outloud scores 1 point. In the event of a tie, no one scores a point. Play continues for a set period of time or until a certain number of points have been reached.

TEACHING TIP: Players may use any number of dice to roll and add at the same time. Include rolling regular 6-sided dice in addition to rolling the 20-sided dice.

"Dear Joanne & Jane,

I love playing the snap games with those cool dice. I'm getting so fast at adding that I beat my older brother! Thanks for making math fun."

A "math fan",
Gregory

FILL 'ER UP

LEVEL: Grade 3 and up

SKILLS: Adding, subtracting, collecting and organizing data in a bar graph, writing number sentences

PLAYERS: 2

EQUIPMENT: One 12-sided die, one 20-sided die, one gameboard per player (see reproducibles)

GETTING STARTED: Each player has a gameboard. The goal is to either fill in a column vertically or horizontally before the other player. Player one rolls the dice and can decide whether to add or subtract the numbers. Player one records this number sentence in the appropriate space. Player two rolls the dice, adds or subtracts, and records the number sentence in the appropriate space. Players continue to alternate turns until one player fills in all numbers 0 - 30 horizontally or fills a vertical column with ten combinations for one number.

EXAMPLE:

								6+3																					
								4+5					20-6		20-4														
4-3			2+2					20-11	8+2			6+7	7+7		9+7				11+9										20+10
1	2	3	4	5	6	7	8	9	10	11	12	13	14	15	16	17	18	19	20	21	22	23	24	25	26	27	28	29	30

VARIATION: If a player rolls a double an additional roll may be taken. Players could multiply and divide the numbers rolled.

OR:

Fill in addition, subtraction for each roll AND if possible fill in multiplication and division combinations.

PUZZLING CHALLENGES

LEVEL: Grade 3 and up

SKILLS: Addition, sums to 60

PLAYERS: 2

EQUIPMENT: Three 20-sided dice per player

GETTING STARTED: Each player rolls the dice and adds the numbers together. The player with the greatest sum receives 2 points.

EXAMPLE:

Player One	**Player Two**
13 + 7 + 3 = 23	12 + 3 + 10 = 25

Player two earns 2 points.

In the event of a tie (each player has the same sum), a tie breaker must be played. Each player rolls their dice again and finds the sum. The first player to roll a sum greater than the tie scores 4 points.

EXAMPLE:

Player One	**Player Two**
4 + 13 + 5 = 22	7 + 9 + 6 = 22
Tie "22"	
5 + 10 + 14 = 29	10 + 12 + 1 = 23

Player one would earn 4 points.

Play continues until one player earns 50 points.

SQUARE DOUBLING

LEVEL: Grade 3 and up

SKILLS: Addition of several addends with regrouping

PLAYERS: 2 - 4

EQUIPMENT: One 10-sided die per player, one gameboard per player (see reproducibles), pencil

GETTING STARTED: Players alternate rolling the die and filling in all twelve squares of their gameboard. The goal of the game is to have the highest total sum of all twelves squares. Each row is calculated separately. In order to have a row counted it must have a double number (ie., two 4's, two 6's, etc.). 2 + 3 + 2 + 8 or 6 + 9 + 1 + 9 can be counted.

If only the top and bottom row include doubling numbers then only these two rows are added for that player's total score. Once a player records their number it cannot be changed. In other words, no erasing.

Beginning with the number in the corner squares the sum for each row is calculated. A row is invalid and may not be calculated for points unless it includes one number that appears twice in that row.

EXAMPLE:

Player One

4. (left column) 2. (right column) 1. (top row) 3. (bottom row)

3	8	1	8
6			2
7			2
3	5	4	5

1. 3 + 8 + 1 + 8 = 20
2. 8 + 2 + 2 + 5 = 17
3. 3 + 5 + 4 + 5 = 17
4. 3 + 6 + 7 + 3 = 19

73

Player one's total sum is 73.

Player Two

4. (left column) 2. (right column) 1. (top row) 3. (bottom row)

6	5	6	8
7			2
3			0
8	1	2	2

1. 6 + 5 + 6 + 8 = 25
2. 8 + 2 + 0 + 2 = 12
3. 8 + 1 + 2 + 2 = 13
4. Row 4 has no doubles - it is not valid.

Player two's total sum is 50.

Players continue to alternate turns for a set period of time. At the end of play, the player with the most points is the winner.

YOUR BOARD OR MINE?

LEVEL: Grade 3 and up

SKILLS: Number recognition, adding two-digit numbers with regrouping, problem solving

PLAYERS: 2

EQUIPMENT: One 20-sided die, one 20-square gameboard with numbers 1 to 20 (see reproducibles), coloured bingo chips or other markers

GETTING STARTED: Each player needs their own gameboard and their own colour of markers. Player one rolls the die and verbalizes the number rolled. Player one may choose to cover up one of their own numbers on their gameboard or to cover up this number on their opponent's board. If they cover one of their opponent's numbers this number is "eliminated" and may not be counted for points at the end of the game. Players attempt to build rows of three or more bingo chips of their own colour in any direction (ie., horizontally, vertically or diagonally).

During the game, players are also trying to prevent their opponents from building their own rows.

Players alternate rolls until the boards are complete or after a set period of time. Each player then adds the face value of all rows covered with three or more markers of their own colour and totals the sum of their rows. The player with the highest sum wins.

VARIATION: Have players avoid getting three squares covered in a row. The player with the least sum wins.

TAKE IT AWAY

LEVEL: Kindergarten to Grade 2

SKILLS: 1 to 1 correspondence of numbers, counting, subtracting

PLAYERS: 2 - 4

EQUIPMENT: K - 1: One 12-sided die and 50 "cube-a-links" per player, container

Grades 1 - 2: one 20-sided die and 100 "cube- a-links" per player, container

GETTING STARTED: To begin both players take 50 or 100 cubes. Player one rolls the die and takes away that number of cubes from his 50 or 100 and places them in a container. Players alternate turns, taking away their cubes. The first player to have only one or no cubes left is the winner.

VARIATION: Players may guesstimate how many rolls it will take to take away all of their cubes. They may share their guesses and see who was closest to their prediction. Players may use a graph to 12 to record their rolls.

SUBTRACT-A-GRAPH

LEVEL: Grade 1 - 3

SKILLS: Subtraction facts to 12, writing numerals, beginning graphing

PLAYERS: 2 - 4

EQUIPMENT: Two 12-sided dice, gameboard (see reproducibles), pencil

GETTING STARTED: Each player has their own gameboard:

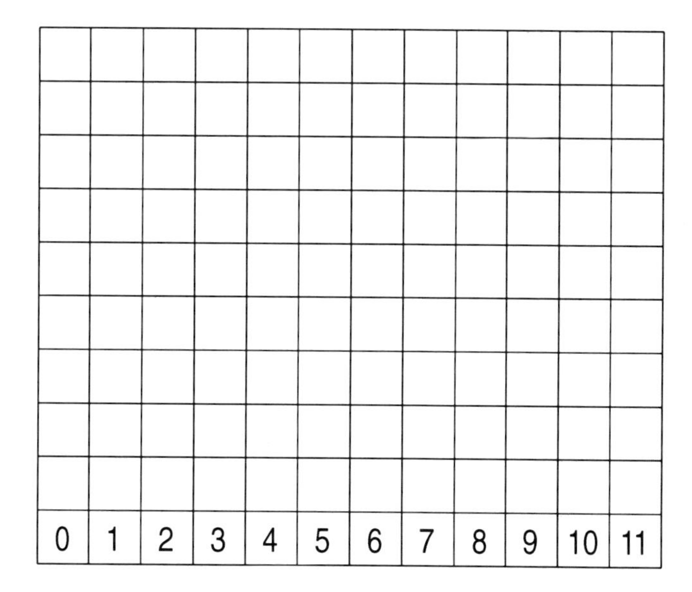

Player one rolls the dice and subtracts the smaller numbered die from the larger numbered die, then writes this equation in the appropriate space on their graph. For instance, if the roll is an 11 and a 2, the player determines the correct difference to be 9 and writes "11 - 2" in the 9 column of their graph. Players alternate turns until one player has one horizontal row filled in.

VARIATION: Have players work in pairs. Play for speed having pairs play against each other.

SUB TRACK

LEVEL:	Grade 1 - 3
SKILLS:	Subtracting from twelve
PLAYERS:	2 - 4
EQUIPMENT:	Two 12-sided dice, gameboard (see reproducibles), pencil

GETTING STARTED: Each player has a gameboard as follows:

0 1 2 3 4 5 6 7 8 9 10 11

X X X

Player one rolls the dice and subtracts the smaller die from the larger die and crosses off the answer on their gameboard. Player two then rolls the dice and subtracts their numbers and crosses off the answer on their gameboard. Players continue to alternate turns. If a player is unable to cross off an answer, they earn a strike, circling the X. Three strikes and the player is out. Play continues until all players are out, or when one player crosses off all of the numbers on their gameboard. If all players strike out, the player with the most numbers crossed off is the winner.

VARIATION: Players create their number lines using a deck of cards (King = 0, Ace = 1, Jack = 11, Queen = 12). Players roll the dice and turn over the answer card. The game ends when one player turns over all of their cards.

FILL THE CARTON

LEVEL: Grade 1 - 3

SKILLS: Subtracting from 12

PLAYERS: 2

EQUIPMENT: Four 12-sided dice, counters, one numbered egg carton per player

GETTING STARTED: Each player has two 12-sided dice, twelve counters and an egg carton. The goal of the game is to place a counter in each section of the numbered egg carton.

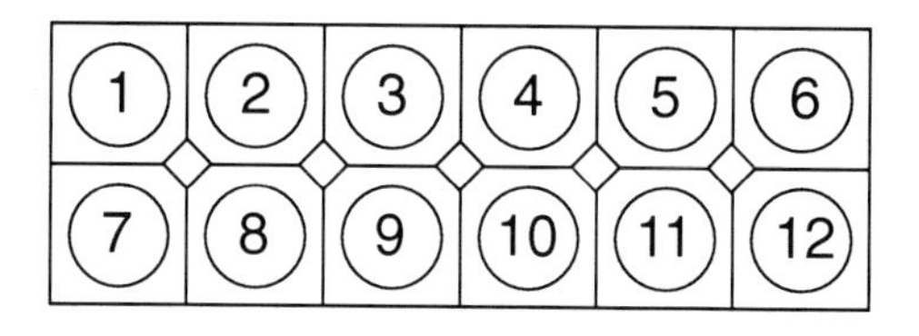

Player one rolls the dice and subtracts the smaller number from the larger determining the difference. The player then places a counter on this number in their egg carton. Player two rolls the dice and repeats the same procedure. To fill in number twelve, players must roll a double. Players continue until one player fills their carton.

VARIATION:

1. Players can add or subtract the dice.
2. Strike Outs – A player can get a strike if they roll a difference already filled in by a counter. Players can get up to three strikes, at which point they stop rolling. If both players strike out, the player with the most numbers filled is the winner.

SUBTRACTION SHAKEDOWN

LEVEL: Grade 2 and up

SKILLS: Subtracting from 20

PLAYERS: 2

EQUIPMENT: One 20-sided die per player, one 12-sided die per player

GETTING STARTED: Each player rolls their two dice and subtracts the smaller number from the larger number. The player with the smallest difference receives 2 points.

EXAMPLE:

Player One	**Player Two**
18 - 9 = 9	14 - 3 = 11

Player one receives 2 points.

In the event of a tie (both players have the same difference), a tie breaker must be played. Each player rolls the dice again to get another difference. The first player to roll a difference less than the tie scores 4 points.

EXAMPLE:

Player One	**Player Two**
16 - 8 = 8	17 - 9 = 8

Tie "8"

Tie Breaker

17 - 10 = 7	14 - 9 = 5

Player two receives 4 points because they have the smallest difference. Play continues until one player earns 50 points.

SUBTRACTION SNAP

LEVEL: Grade 2 and up

SKILLS: Immediate recall, subtracting from 20

PLAYERS: 2 (equal skill level)

EQUIPMENT: One 20-sided die, one 10-sided die

GETTING STARTED: At the same time, each player rolls one of the die. Players must subtract the smaller number from the larger number. The first player to say the correct answer outloud scores 1 point. In the event of a tie, no one scores a point. Play continues for a set period of time or until a certain number of points have been reached.

REACH FOR THE TOP

LEVEL: Grade 1 - 3

SKILLS: Adding to 18, subtracting from 9, graphing

PLAYERS: Solitaire or 2

EQUIPMENT: Two 10-sided dice, gameboard (see reproducibles)

GETTING STARTED: Each player has a gameboard. The goal is to fill in a column (10 up) in as few rolls as possible. The player rolls the dice and adds the two numbers to find a sum. If this sum fits on the graph it is filled in. The player may also subtract the two numbers to find a difference, which is also recorded. The player continues to roll and record answers until one column is filled in.

EXAMPLE:

	2 - 1									
	3 - 2									
	5 - 4						8 - 1			
	1 - 0						5 + 2		8 + 1	
	1 + 0			8 - 4	3 + 2		9 - 2	8 - 0	5 + 4	
	1 - 0		2 + 1	5 - 1	7 - 2		9 - 2	8 + 0	7 + 2	
8 - 8	1 + 0		5 - 2	6 - 2	8 - 3	5 + 1	8 - 1	7 + 1	5 + 4	
8 - 8	5 - 4		8 - 5	8 - 4	4 + 1	7 - 1	9 - 2	9 - 1	8 + 1	
4 - 4	4 - 3	8 - 6	4 - 1	4 - 0	9 - 4	3 + 3	5 + 2	4 + 4	9 - 0	
3 - 3	9 - 8	7 - 5	5 - 2	4 + 0	8 - 3	9 - 3	3 + 4	6 + 2	0 + 9	9 + 1
0	1	2	3	4	5	6	7	8	9	10

WHAT'S MISSING?

LEVEL: Grade 3 and up

SKILLS: Identifying the missing addend

PLAYERS: 2

EQUIPMENT: One 20-sided die, one 10-sided die, paper, pencil

GETTING STARTED: Player one rolls the 10-sided die and then rolls the 20-sided die (ie., 3 and 17) and calls out the math sentence "3 + _ = 17". Player two must determine what the missing addend is and call out the answer (ie., "14"). If the answer is correct, the player receives 1 point. If the answer is incorrect, the other player can give their answer and if correct they earn 1 point. Players alternate turns. Play continues until one player reaches 20 points.

VARIATION: To increase the level of difficulty have players roll three multi-sided dice (ie., 4, 11 and 18). Player one could create the math sentence "4 + 11 + ___ = 18". Player two must determine what the missing addend is and call out the answer (ie., "3").

PEEK A BOO

LEVEL: Grade 3 and up

SKILLS: Identifying the missing addend

PLAYERS: 2

EQUIPMENT: Three 12-sided dice, margarine tub

GETTING STARTED: Player one secretly sets up an equation for player two. This is done by rolling one die and placing it on top of the margarine tub (1). A number on a second die that is greater than the die shown on the top of the tub is then chosen (2). Player one must determine the missing addend, and place the die with the number underneath the margarine tub (3). Player two can now look at the equation that player one has arranged. Player two must predict the missing addend by looking at the die on top of the tub and the die that is set aside and visible. They may then "peek" under the tub to see if their answer is correct. If so, players reverse roles. If the answer is incorrect, player one sets up a second equation. Players collect points each time they get a correct answer or when they stump an opponent.

EXAMPLE:

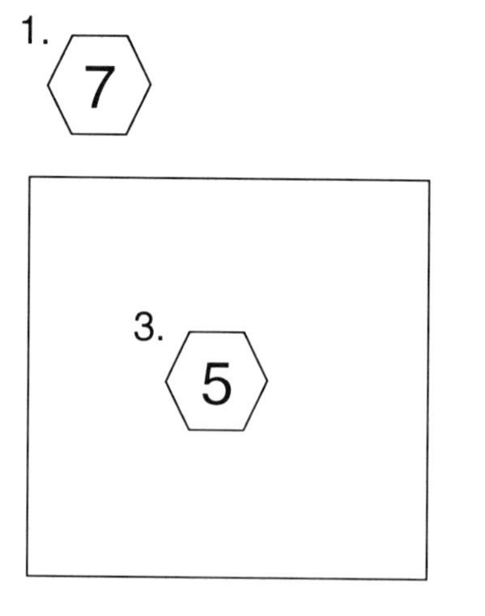

To calculate the answer player could do the following:

$7 + \_\_ = 12$

or: $12 - 7 = \_\_$

or: $12 - \_\_ = 7$

PEEK A BOO RACE

LEVEL: Grade 4 and up

SKILLS: Identifying the missing addend, immediate recall

PLAYERS: 2 (equal skill level)

EQUIPMENT: Six 12-sided dice, margarine tub

GETTING STARTED: Follow the same game directions and rules as Peek A Boo, with the added variation of speed. Each player secretly sets up their own equation for their opponent. One player says "Go" and both players attempt to solve the other's equation at the same time. The first player to correctly solve their opponent's problem scores 1 point. The first player to score 10 points is the winner.

SOUNDS DICEY

LEVEL: Grade 3 and up

SKILLS: Addition, subtraction, odd/even

PLAYERS: 2

EQUIPMENT: One 20-sided die, pencil, paper

GETTING STARTED: Each player starts with 50 points. Player one rolls the die. If the number is even, this number is added to their 50 points. If the number rolled is odd, this number is subtracted from their 50 points. Players continue rolling and continue to add or subtract from their accumulated points until one player reaches 200.

Note: If a player goes below zero, they freeze at zero until an even number is rolled.

CROSS OVERS

LEVEL: Grade 2 and up

SKILLS: Adding, subtracting, missing addends

PLAYERS: 2 - 4

EQUIPMENT: One 10-sided die, one gameboard (see reproducibles) per player, pencil

GETTING STARTED: The goal of the game is to equal the total of 20 in either direction on the gameboard. One player is selected to roll the die for the round. The die is rolled and each player records that number somewhere on the gameboard. Four more rolls are taken to fill the gameboard for a total of five rolls. Once a number has been recorded into a particular space, it cannot be erased.

Using either addition or addition and subtraction, each row is calculated and compared to the other player's totals.

Players earn 5 points for any row that equals 20 exactly, 2 points if their total is two less or greater than twenty, and 1 point for being closer to twenty than any other player for that row.

Play continues for a set period of time. The player with the most points wins.

EXAMPLE: Rolls: 4, 6, 9, 2, 1

Row 1: 4 + 6 + 9 = 19

Row 2: 2 + 6 + 1 = 9

	2	
4	6	9
	1	

To determine if player one earns points on Rows 1 and 2 they must compare to player two's board.

VARIATION: Allow mixed operations (ie., players may apply any operation between the numbers to reach the total of 20).

METRE MADNESS

LEVEL: Grade 3 and up

SKILLS: Adding and subtracting to 100, odd and even numbers

PLAYERS: 2 - 4

EQUIPMENT: One 10-sided die, metre stick, coloured marker for each player

GETTING STARTED: Each player begins by placing their marker on the 50 cm. mark of the metre stick. The goal is to be the first player to reach either 0 or 100. Each player in turn rolls the die. If the number is odd, the player subtracts that number and moves left (towards zero) on the metre stick. If the number is even, the player adds and moves that number to the right on the metre stick. The first player to land on 0 or 100 is the winner.

EXAMPLE: Player one rolls 8, records 50 + 8 = 58. Player one's second roll is 7, records 58 - 7 = 51, etc.

40 41 42 43 44 45 46 47 48 49 50 51 52 53 54 55 56 57 58 59 60

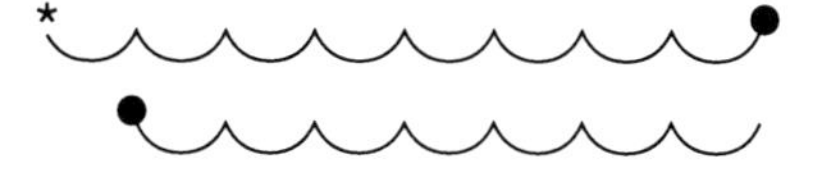

VARIATION: Have students record their rolls. Students may also tally the number of rolls they required to land on 0 or 100 for that round.

EVEN OR ODDS?

LEVEL: Grade 3 and up

SKILLS: Identifying odd and even numbers, adding and regrouping

PLAYERS: 2 - 4

EQUIPMENT: Two 10, 12, and 20-sided dice, paper, pencil

GETTING STARTED: To start, each player rolls a 20-sided die. The player who rolled the highest number begins the round.

In round one, player one rolls all six multi-sided dice at once and all EVEN numbered dice are put aside and added together for a total sum. This sum is recorded on paper for player one's first round.

EXAMPLE: Roll = 2, 7, 10, 4, 15, 19

Player one records 2 + 10 + 4 = 16

Player two now takes their turn.

For round two, player one rolls all six dice at once and all ODD numbered dice are put aside and added together for a total sum. This sum is added to player one's previous total from round one.

EXAMPLE: Roll = 9, 2, 5, 8, 12, 11

Player one records 9 + 5 + 11 = 25

Player one's accumulative total = 41. (16 + 25)

Players continue alternating turns until one player reaches a score of 100 points.

SUM IT UP

LEVEL: Grade 4 and up

SKILLS: Adding of three digit numbers

PLAYERS: 2 - 4, or teacher vs. whole class

EQUIPMENT: One 10-sided die, paper, pencil

GETTING STARTED: One player will roll the die for the group. Each player makes a gameboard as follows:

```
  __ __ __
  __ __ __
+ __ __ __
__________
```

The goal of this game is to make the largest sum possible. The die is rolled. Each player puts the number into their gameboard (ie., if a two is rolled players could place that number in the one's place. If a nine is rolled, it could logically be placed in the hundred's place).

Player One	Player Two	Player Three
__ 5 __	__ 8 __	9 __ __
9 __ __	9 __ 5	8 __ __
+ 8 __ 2	+ __ __ 2	+ __ 5 2

Each time the die is rolled the players decide where that number will go on their gameboard. After nine rolls, players add up their numbers. The player with the largest sum receives 1 point for the round. If more than one player gets the same sum, each player receives a point. For this round 2, 5, 9, 8, 1, 3, 4, 2, 6 were rolled and were placed into the grids by the players as follows:

Player One	Player Two	Player Three
6 5 1	3 8 1	9 1 4
9 4 3	9 4 5	8 2 3
+ 8 2 2	+ 6 2 2	+ 6 5 2
2 4 1 6	1 9 4 8	2 3 8 9

Player number one scores 1 point, and can roll the next nine numbers.

VARIATION: Multiplication:

```
  __ __            __ __ __
X __ __     OR   X __ __ __
_______          __________
```

GUESS YOUR PLACE

LEVEL: Grade 3 and up

SKILLS: Addition with regrouping, estimating

PLAYERS: 2 - 4

EQUIPMENT: Two 20-sided dice, paper, pencil

GETTING STARTED: Each player rolls two 20-sided dice and creates the largest number in place value. Before rolling the player predicts whether the number will be a tens, hundreds or thousands number. If the player is correct, this number is recorded for that round. Players calculate the sum of their totals after five rounds and the player with the greatest sum wins.

EXAMPLE: **Player one** rolls: 6, 18

The largest number would be 618. If the player predicted hundreds, then 618 is recorded as points. If the player made an incorrect prediction, no points are earned.

Player two rolls: 11, 15

The largest number would be 1511. If the player predicted thousands, then 1511 is recorded as points. If the player made an incorrect prediction, no points are earned.

Section III

Multiplication & Division

MULTI BREAKER

LEVEL: Grade 5 and up

SKILLS: Multiplying to 144

PLAYERS: 2

EQUIPMENT: Two 12-sided dice per player

GETTING STARTED: Each player rolls their dice and multiplies the two numbers together. The player with the greatest product receives 2 points.

EXAMPLE:

Player One	**Player Two**
9 x 7 = 63	4 x 8 = 32

Player one receives 2 points.

In the event of a tie (both players have the same product), a tie breaker must be played. Each player rolls the dice again to get a new product. The first player to roll a product greater than the "tie" wins 4 points.

EXAMPLE:

Player One	**Player Two**
4 x 9 = 36	3 x 12 = 36

Tie "36"

Tie Breaker

5 x 5 = 25	7 x 6 = 42

Player two receives 4 points.

Play continues until one player scores 50 points.

FAIR GAME MULTIPLICATION

LEVEL: Grade 4 and up

SKILLS: Multiplying to 100, odd and even numbers

PLAYERS: 2

EQUIPMENT: Two 10-sided dice per player, one regular die

GETTING STARTED: Each player rolls their two 10-sided dice and multiplies them together. Player number one rolls the regular die to determine who wins the point.

1, 3, 5 - odd roll - lower product wins the point

2, 4, 6 - even roll - higher product wins the point

Players continue to roll the dice and multiply them. Players alternate the roll of the regular die. If the players roll equal products, each player receives a point. The first player to score 20 points is the winner.

VARIATION: Players must verbalize their products AND round their answer off to the nearest ten, before determining the winner.

MULTIPLICATION SCRAMBLE

LEVEL: Grade 4 and up

SKILLS: Recall of multiplication facts to 144

PLAYERS: 2 or solitaire

EQUIPMENT: Two 12-sided dice per player, gameboard (see reproducibles), pencil

GETTING STARTED: Each player has their own gameboard.

The goal of the game is to fill in every line on the gameboard. Each player rolls two dice and multiplies them together. Players write down their products on the appropriate lines on their gameboards (ie., 4 x 7 = 28 would go on the line beside 20 - 29). The first player to get all lines on their gameboard filled is the winner.

EXAMPLE:

	Player One	**Player Two**
0 - 9	________	________
10 - 19	________	________
20 - 29	4 x 7 = 28	________
30 - 39	9 x 4 = 36	5 x 6 = 30
40 - 49	9 x 5 = 45	6 x 8 = 48
50 - 59	________	________
60 - 69	________	________
70 - 79	________	________
80 - 89	________	________
90 - 99	________	10 x 9 = 90
100 - 109	________	________
110 - 119	________	________
120 - 129	________	________
130 - 139	________	________
140 - 149	________	________

Turn 1: Player one rolls 4 and 7 (4 x 7 = 28)

Turn 2: Player two rolls 5 and 6 (5 x 6 = 30)

VARIATION: To work on multiplication facts to 100, use two 10-sided dice per player. Use a gameboard up to 100 - 109.

MULTIPLICATION SNAP

LEVEL:	Grade 5 and up
SKILLS:	Immediate recall, multiplying to 100 / 144
PLAYERS:	2 (equal skill level)
EQUIPMENT:	Two 10-sided dice or two 12-sided dice
GETTING STARTED:	At the same time each player rolls one die. Players must multiply the two numbers. The first player to say the correct product outloud scores 1 point. In the event of a tie, no one scores a point. Play continues for a set period of time or until a certain number of points have been reached.

VARIATION:

Have players roll an additional regular die and multiply three numbers at the same time. Player may need paper and pencils to calculate their products before verbalizing their answers outloud.

Players may use different strategies to calculate their answer.

ie., 4 x 8 x 7 = 56 x 4 = 224
↕
50 x 4 = 200
6 x 4 = 24

OR: 4 x 8 x 7 = 32 x 7 = 224
↕
30 x 7 = 210
2 x 7 = 14

FIGURE IT OUT!

LEVEL:	Grade 5 and up
SKILLS:	Multiplying three factors
PLAYERS:	2 - 4
EQUIPMENT:	Two 20-sided dice, one 10-sided die, paper, pencil
GETTING STARTED:	One player rolls the 20-sided dice. Players multiply these two numbers to get a product. The same player rolls the 10-sided die. Players multiply this number with the previous product. The first player to call out the correct answer scores 1 point.
EXAMPLE:	Roll 1: 20 and 15; 20 x 15 = 300
	Roll 2: 7; 7 x 300 = 2100
	Players alternate rolling the dice. Play continues until one player scores 20 points. Players may use pencil and paper or a calculator for their calculations.
VARIATION:	All players that get the correct answer score 1 point.

THE BIG ROUND UP

LEVEL: Grade 5 and up

SKILLS: Multiplying to 144, rounding off to the nearest 10

PLAYERS: 2

EQUIPMENT: Two 12-sided dice, paper, pencil, gameboard (see reproducibles)

GETTING STARTED: Each player has their own gameboard

10 20 30 40 50 60 70 80 90 100 110 120 130 140

The goal of the game is for players to cross off all the numbers on their gameboard. The first player to do so is the winner. Player one rolls the dice and multiplies them. The product is then rounded off to the nearest ten.

EXAMPLE: Roll 6 and 12, 6 x 12 = 72
Round off to nearest ten = 70
Player crosses 70 off of their gameboard

Player two may then take their turn. Players alternate rolls, crossing numbers off their gameboards. If a player cannot cross off a number, play simply continues to the next player. The first player to cross off all of their numbers is the winner.

VARIATION: When doubles are rolled, an extra turn is taken.

A ROUND OF DICE

LEVEL: Grade 5 and up

SKILLS: Multiplying four factors, rounding off to nearest 100

PLAYERS: 1 or more

EQUIPMENT: Four 10-sided dice, paper, pencil, gameboard

GETTING STARTED: Each player makes their own gameboard. The goal of the game is for players to cross off all numbers on their board. The first player to do so is the winner. Player one rolls the dice, multiplies them and says the product outloud. This number is then rounded off to the nearest hundred and crossed off their gameboard.

EXAMPLE: 7 x 4 x 1 x 9 = 252, 300 is crossed off

0 100 200 300 400 500 600 700

If that number has already been crossed off, that turn is complete. Player two may then take their turn. Players alternate rolls until one player has crossed all numbers off their gameboard.

ON TARGET

LEVEL: Grade 5 and up

SKILLS: Multiplying facts to 100

PLAYERS: 2

EQUIPMENT: Two 10-sided dice, gameboard (see reproducibles), pencil

GETTING STARTED: Players use one gameboard.

					TARGET NUMBER					
	x		=		10		=		x	
	x		=		20		=		x	
	x		=		30		=		x	
	x		=		40		=		x	
	x		=		50		=		x	
	x		=		60		=		x	
	x		=		70		=		x	
	x		=		80		=		x	
	x		=		90		=		x	
	x		=		100		=		x	

The goal of the game is for players to create a product as close to the Target Number without going over, on all ten lines. Player one rolls the die and decides where to put that number on their side of the gameboard. This number will be multiplied with another and the product compared to the Target Number at the completion of the rolls. Player two rolls the die and goes through the same procedure. Players continue to alternate turns until all their spaces are filled in.

THEN:

Players multiply their numbers and fill in the products. The products are compared to the Target Number. Whichever player has the closest number scores the point for that line. In the event of a tie (both products on a line are equal), both players score a point. Players compare their numbers to the Target Number on all ten lines and points are calculated. The player with the most points wins.

THREE FOR ME

LEVEL: Grade 5 and up

SKILLS: Multiplying to 144

PLAYERS: 2

EQUIPMENT: Two 12-sided dice, multiplication table (see reproducibles), bingo chips - two colours (or other markers)

GETTING STARTED: Players use one gameboard. Each player chooses a colour of bingo chips. Player one rolls the dice, multiplies them, and places their chips on possible combinations of that product.

EXAMPLE: Player one rolls 6 and 4, and places chips on combinations for 24, (ie., 6 x 4 and 4 x 6 and 3 x 8 and 8 x 3 and 12 x 2 and 2 x 12).

	1	2	3	4	5	6	7	8	9	10	11	12
1	1	2	3	4	5	6	7	8	9	10	11	12
2	2	4	6	8	10	12	14	16	18	20	22	24
3	3	6	9	12	15	18	21	24	27	30	33	36
4	4	8	12	16	20	24	28	32	36	40	44	48
5	5	10	15	20	25	30	35	40	45	50	55	60
6	6	12	18	24	30	36	42	48	54	60	66	72
7	7	14	21	28	35	42	49	56	63	70	77	84
8	8	16	24	32	40	48	56	64	72	80	88	96
9	9	18	27	36	45	54	63	72	81	90	99	108
10	10	20	30	40	50	60	70	80	90	100	110	120
11	11	22	33	44	55	66	77	88	99	110	121	132
12	12	24	36	48	60	72	84	96	108	120	132	144

Player one verbalizes that their turn is over. Player two may then cover any missed combinations with their bingo chips. Player two then rolls 7 and 12 and puts chips on combinations for 84.

Players alternate rolling the dice and placing chips on the board. The goal is for players to get three chips in a row either horizontally, vertically, or diagonally. If a player gets three in a row, they take them off the board and they become “keepers”. They will be used at the end of the game to calculate the player’s final score.

Capturing a Player’s Chip: If a player rolls a number that is already occupied by the opposition, they can capture it. They take their opponent’s chip and replace it with their own. The captured chip is kept by the roller, and becomes a “keeper”. It will be used at the end of the game to determine their final score.

Determining the Winner: After a set period of time the game ends. To determine the score, keepers are counted as follows:

Keepers of the player’s own colour = 2 points each
Keepers of the opponent’s colour = 5 points each
Own chips left on the board = 1 point each

The player with the most points wins.

GUESSTIMATE THOSE PRODUCTS

LEVEL: Grade 4 and up

SKILLS: Multiplication of 3 one-digit numbers

PLAYERS: 3 (equal skill level)

EQUIPMENT: Three 10-sided dice, calculator, paper, pencil

GETTING STARTED: The goal of the game is for players to estimate the product of the three dice. One player is the roller and the timer. The roller rolls the dice and begins counting off between eight to ten seconds once the dice have come to rest. The other two players quickly estimate the product of the three numbers rolled. They must record their estimates on paper before their time is up. Once the time is up the roller uses the calculator to determine the actual product. Players calculate the difference between their estimate and the true product. Whoever has the closest estimate to the actual product earns 1 point. Both players can earn a point if they are equally as close.

Rolls or "Roles" are rotated so a new player becomes the "Roller/Timer" each round.

Play continues for a set period of time. The player with the most points is the winner.

EXAMPLE: Rolls: 4, 6, 3

Product = 72

Player One	**Player Two**
Estimated and recorded "70"	Estimated and recorded "78"
Player one's difference is 2	Player two's difference is 6

Player one's difference is less and would earn 1 point for that round.

TEACHING TIP: Encourage players to verbalize their estimation strategies after each round.

VARIATION: Use 12-sided or 20-sided dice.

GO FORTH AND MULTIPLY

LEVEL:	Grade 3 and up
SKILLS:	Multiplying to 60
PLAYERS:	2
EQUIPMENT:	One 10-sided die and one regular die per player
GETTING STARTED:	Each player rolls their dice and multiplies the two numbers together. The player with the greatest product receives one point.

EXAMPLE:

Player One	**Player Two**
8 x 3 = 24	1 x 9 = 9

Player one receives 1 point.

In the event of a tie (ie., both players have the same product), a tie breaker must be played. Each player rolls the dice again to get a new product. The first player to roll a product greater than the "tie" wins 4 points.

EXAMPLE:

Player One	**Player Two**
3 x 6 = 18	9 x 2 = 18

Tie "18"

Tie Breaker

2 x 5 = 10	6 x 6 = 36

Player two receives 4 points. Play continues until one player scores 50 points.

VARIATION: Players round off their products to the nearest ten before comparing to their partner (ie., player one rolls 7 x 6 = 42, and rounds this down to 40).

DARING DIVISION

LEVEL: Grade 4 and up

SKILLS: Dividing, multiplying, estimating, mental math

PLAYERS: 2

EQUIPMENT: Two 20-sided dice, cards Ace - 9 (Ace = 1), King (King = 0), calculator, paper, pencil

GETTING STARTED: One player rolls the dice and makes a two, three or four-digit number in place value. Player one now flips a card off the top of the deck. Both players must mentally calculate and estimate the quotient as accurately as possible. The player whose estimation is closest to the quotient receives 1 point. If one player's answer is exact, that player earns 1 bonus point.

In the event of a tie (ie., both players respond correctly at the same time), both players earn 1 point.

Calculators, paper and pencil may be used to check answers for accuracy, after they have been given.

EXAMPLE: Roll: 16, 15

Number = 1615

Card = 6

1615 ÷ 6

Player one estimates and verbalizes "275".

Player two estimates and verbalizes "260".

The answer equals 269 remainder 1.

Player one earns 1 point.

Section IV

Mixed Operations

COMBO MR. WOLF

LEVEL: Grade 3 and up

SKILLS: Mixed operations (+, –, x, ÷), problem-solving

PLAYERS: Solitaire or cooperative pair

EQUIPMENT: One 12-sided die, cards Ace - Queen (Ace = 1, Jack = 11, Queen = 12)

GETTING STARTED: Player builds a clock with cards Ace - Queen as follows:

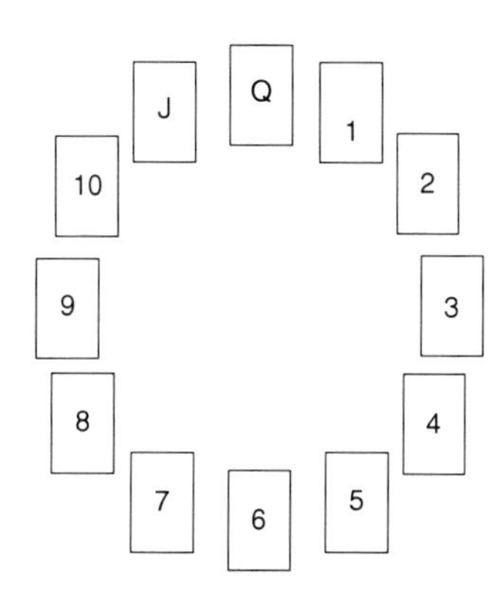

The goal of the game is to take as few rolls as possible to remove all cards from the clock. The player rolls the die and places it in the centre of their clock. This number becomes the target number (ie., player rolls a 9 and may now select either a two, three, or four card combination that equals a target roll of 9). The player may add, subtract, multiply or divide to reach the target number.

EXAMPLE:

Roll 1 = 5 Removes 12 - 7 = 5

Roll 2 = 3 Removes (11 - 10) + 2 = 3

Roll 3 = 9 Removes (8 + 4) - 3 = 9

Roll 4 = 3 Removes 9 - 6 = 3

Roll 5 = 5 Removes 5 x 1 = 5

Clock removed in five rolls.

If a player is unable to remove any cards to match the target, they tally it as a roll. The player re-rolls for a new target number.

Play for the round is completed when all cards have been removed.

SPEEDY GRAPHING

LEVEL: Grade 4 and up

SKILLS: Multi operations (+, -, x, ÷), graphing

PLAYERS: 4: 2 vs. 2

EQUIPMENT: Two 10-sided dice, gameboard (see reproducibles), pencil

GETTING STARTED: Each team shares two 10-sided dice and one gameboard. When one person says "Go" all teams begin to roll their dice. Players may fill in up to four squares on their gameboard that equal a combination of the numbers rolled. For example, 3 and 6 are rolled. Players may colour in a 9 square (3 + 6), a 3 square (6 - 3), an 18 square (6 x 3), and a 2 square (6 ÷ 3). Each team continues to roll and fill in their gameboard as quickly as possible. The first team of players to fill in one whole row of squares either vertically or horizontally on their gameboard wins.

VARIATION: Players write the equations in the appropriate squares when recording their answers.

"Dear Joanne & Jane,

I liked your presentation. I learned lots of fun games to play. You guys are terrific. Other kids would like to learn and play those games. I'm waiting for your next book to come out. I'm excited to read it. Thanks for coming."

from L.K.
Grade 4

TANGLE WITH TWENTY

LEVEL: Grade 3 and up

SKILLS: Multi operations (+, –, x, ÷)

PLAYERS: 2 or teacher vs. whole class

EQUIPMENT: Two 10-sided dice per player, gameboard (see reproducibles), pencil

GETTING STARTED: Each player has two 10-sided dice and a gameboard.

0 1 2 3 4 5 6 7 8 9 10 11 12 13 14 15 16 17 18 19 20

X X X

The goal of the game is to cross off as many numbers as possible before getting three strikes. Player one rolls the dice. Player one can +, -, x, or ÷ the two dice. Player one can choose only one combination to take into their gameboard.

EXAMPLE:

Step 1

Player one rolls 8 and 6 and possible combinations could include $8 + 6 = 14$
$8 - 6 = 2$
$8 \times 6 = 48$

Player one decides which combination they will take into their gameboard.

Step 2

Player one chooses 14, and may now cross off two numbers that make that combination, such as 9 and 5 ($9 + 5 = 14$), 2 and 7 ($2 \times 7 = 14$), 18 and 4 ($18 - 4 = 14$), etc.

Player two rolls the dice and follows the same procedure on their own gameboard. If a player cannot cross off any combination of numbers to match their roll they receive a strike, circling the X. After a player gets three strikes they stop rolling and wait until their opponent can no longer roll. Players compare their gameboards to see who crossed off the most numbers. The player with the most numbers crossed off is the winner. In the event of a tie, players can calculate the sum of their open numbers. The smallest sum wins.

VARIATION: Add another 10-sided die and cross off up to three numbers at a time.

1000 BULLSEYE

LEVEL: Grade 3 and up

SKILLS: Adding to 20, multiplying to 100

PLAYERS: 2 or solitaire

EQUIPMENT: Two 10-sided dice, paper, pencil

GETTING STARTED: The goal of the game is to be the first player to reach 1000 exactly. Each player in turn rolls the dice. Players may either add them together to get a sum or multiply them to get a product. Player one rolls the dice and records their choice of sum or product. Player two then takes a turn and records their sum or product. Players alternate turns keeping a running total. Players may take a bonus roll if they hit a hundred exactly (ie., 100, 200, 300, etc.) or roll a double (ie., 2 and 2, 4 and 4, etc.). Strategy will come into play as players try to get bonus rolls by choosing a sum or product which would result in hitting a hundred exactly. Play continues until one player hits 1000 on the "bullseye."

VARIATION: Solitaire: players can play individually. The number of rolls to 1000 can be calculated.

MULTI OPERATION BLACKOUT

LEVEL: Grade 4 and up

SKILLS: Multi operations (+, -, x, ÷)

PLAYERS: 4: 2 teams of 2

EQUIPMENT: Three 10-sided dice, two hundred boards (see reproducibles), bingo chips or other markers

GETTING STARTED: The goal of the game is to be the first team to cover every number on their hundreds chart. Team one rolls the three dice. Players figure out all of the combinations they can make with the three numbers using all operations.

EXAMPLE: Roll 6, 9, 2

6 + 9 + 2 = 17
(9 - 6) + 2 = 5
(9 x 6) + 2 = 56
(6 x 2) - 9 = 3
etc.

Player may cover up numbers 17, 5, 56, 3, etc.

For each answer, each team may cover that number on their hundred board. Teams are allowed a maximum of three minutes per roll. Team two then rolls the three dice and repeats the same procedure. Teams alternate turns until one team successfully covers up all of their numbers.

Note: Players could keep a written record of their rolls and multi operation sequences.

VARIATION: At the end of a team's time limit the opposing team can "capture" any number combinations that their opponents have missed (ie., in above example team one misses 56. Team two covers 56 on their gameboard as a capture).

VARIATION: Use 20-sided dice.

TARGET SUM

LEVEL: Grade 4 and up

SKILLS: Mixed operations (+, -, x, ÷)

PLAYERS: Group of 5

EQUIPMENT: Five 12-sided dice per player, paper, pencil

GETTING STARTED: Each player rolls one die. These rolls are added to get a Target Sum for the group.

ie., 2 + 4 + 8 + 9 + 9
Target Sum for group = 32

The goal for each player is then to roll their five dice and reach the Target Sum (32 in this example). Players may do this using any combination of operations (+, -, x, ÷). All numbers a player rolls must be used. Each number is used only once in that combination. Each player can score 1 point per round if they can reach the Target Sum with their numbers. After the round, players start again by each rolling one die and establishing a new Target Sum. Players then re-roll their five dice and try to reach the new Target Sum. The game ends after a set period of time. The player with the most points wins.

Bonus Points: If a player can create more than one math sentence to hit the target sum, they score an extra point.

VARIATION: The class can be divided into groups and compete against one another. The teacher can roll the Target Sum. Each group rolls five dice and works together to try to reach the Target Sum. After a set number of rounds, groups total their points. The group with the most points wins.

CUT IT OUT!

LEVEL: Grade 3 and up

SKILLS: Mixed operations (+, -, x, ÷)

PLAYERS: 2 - 3

EQUIPMENT: One 20-sided die, cards Ace - Queen (Ace = 1, Jack = 11, Queen = 12), paper, pencil

GETTING STARTED: The goal of the game is to equal the target number by manipulating the three cards cut from the deck. Each player "cuts the deck" and selects three cards. Players alternate rolling the die. The number rolled is the target number each player attempts to reach by manipulating their three cards. Players look at their own three cards and figure out all of the combinations they can make with their three numbers using all operations. All players who verbalize correct math sentences that equal the target roll, earn 1 point. Players may also record their math sentences on paper.

EXAMPLE: Roll = 16

Player One

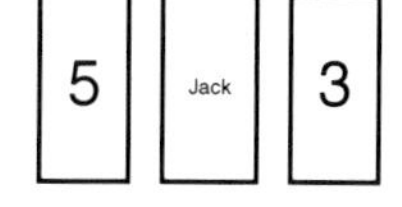

(11 - 3) + 5 = 13

Player Two

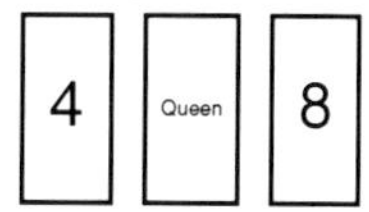

(12 + 8) - 4 = 16

Player two verbalizes "twelve plus eight equals twenty, minus four equals sixteen" and earns 1 point. If a player cannot reach the target roll a new number is rolled and new cards are "cut" from the deck.

Play continues for a set period of time. The player with the most points wins.

VARIATION: Players are allowed to use one, two or three cards to reach the target number. In the above example, player one would earn points for adding their Jack plus 5 card to equal sixteen (ie., 11 + 5 = 16) and leave the 3 card for the next round.

FREEZING FORTY-FIVE

LEVEL: Grade 3 and up

SKILLS: Mixed operations (+, -, x, ÷)

PLAYERS: 2 - 4

EQUIPMENT: Two 12-sided dice, paper, pencil

GETTING STARTED: Player one rolls the dice and may choose to add, subtract, multiply or divide the numbers rolled. The goal is to reach the total of 'forty-five' in three rolls. A player may choose to "freeze" after the first or second roll, record their number and their play is over. Players continue to take turns and the player closest to forty-five for each round earns 1 point. If a player reaches forty-five exactly, they earn 5 points. The first player to score 30 points is the winner.

EXAMPLE: **PLAYER ONE:**

1st Roll: Player one rolls 8 and 7 and chooses to add the numbers for a total of 15.

2nd Roll: Player one rolls 3 and 5 and chooses to multiply the numbers for a total of 15. Player one now adds the first and second roll to equal 30.

3rd Roll: Player one rolls 3 and 9 and chooses to add the numbers for a total of 12. Player one now adds the previous total of 30 to 12 for a final sum of 42.

Player two takes their turn and at the completion of their roll(s), both players compare answers. The player closest to forty-five earns 1 point.

CARD TARGET

LEVEL: Grade 4 and up

SKILLS: Mixed operations (+, -, x, ÷), problem solving, missing addends, minuends, factors, divisors

PLAYERS: 4 - 6

EQUIPMENT: One 12-sided die, cards Ace - King (Ace = 1, Jack = 11, Queen = 12, King = 0)

GETTING STARTED: Each player is dealt five cards, the rest of the deck is placed face down for the next round. A die is rolled to establish a target number for the round. Players must use a minimum of three cards, and any operation to target the number rolled. Each card must be used once, and only once to reach the target. Once the die is rolled, all players look at their cards and attempt to target the number. Any player who is able to do so, places their cards down, verbalizes their math sentence, and replenishes their hand. The cards placed down to reach the target number are put aside and will be counted for points at the end of the game.

Players who have targeted the number, replenish their hands and a new TARGET is rolled for the next round. Players who were unable to reach the TARGET keep the same cards - they do not replenish their cards until they reach a target during a future round.

WHEN A TARGET NUMBER CANNOT BE MADE BY ANY PLAYER IN THE FIRST ROUND, all players must select one card from their hand and pass it to the player on their right. All players now look at their new combination of cards to attempt to target the number. Any player who is now able to reach the target number using at least three of their cards, places their cards down as outlined above.

WHEN A TARGET NUMBER CANNOT BE MADE BY ANY PLAYER IN THE SECOND ROUND, all players must select one card from their hand and pass it to the player on their right. All players now look at their new combination of cards to attempt to target the number. Any player who is now able to reach the target number using at least three of their cards, places their cards down as outlined above.

If at this point no player can target the number a new target number is rolled and a new round of play begins.

After a set period of time players count up the number of cards they have placed aside. The player with the most cards is the winner.

VARIATION:

Players may choose an operation (ie., addition, subtraction, multiplication or division) prior to rolling the target number. Players must use that operation at least once while attempting to target the number with their cards.

TEAM WORK

LEVEL: Grade 4 and up

SKILLS: Mixed operations (+, -, x, ÷), exponents (optional)

PLAYERS: 2 vs. 2

EQUIPMENT: One 12-sided die, cards Ace - King (Ace = 1, Jack = 11, Queen = 12, King = 0)

GETTING STARTED: The goal of the game is to equal the target number by placing down the last card in a card combination. Each player is dealt five cards. Players on the same team may look at the cards in their partner's hands. One player from each team rolls the die and the team with the highest number rolls the target number and chooses to begin or not to begin the game.

Team A Player One	**Team B Player One**
Team A Player Two	**Team B Player Two**

TEAM A

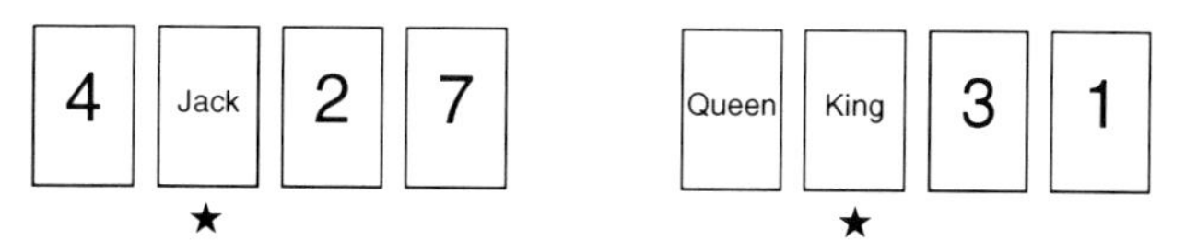

TEAM B

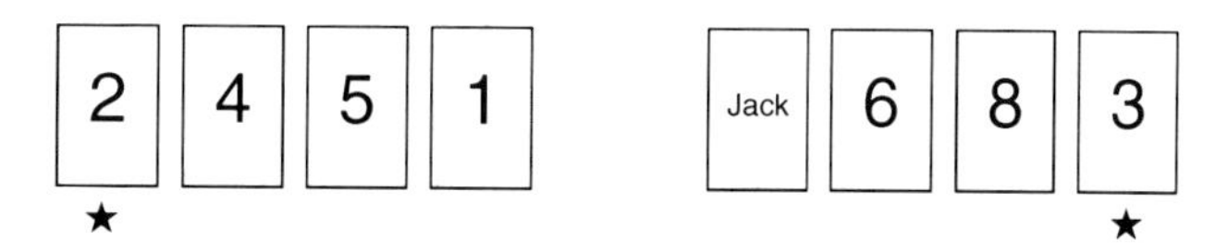

Team A begins by rolling "9" for the target number. Player one on Team A begins by looking at their cards and placing a Jack down (= 11). Players do not replenish their hands with new cards. Player one on Team B places a 2 down, verbalizes "11 - 2 = 9" and collects both cards, placing them aside for points. Player two on Team B chooses to begin and lays down a 3. Player two on Team A places down a King and verbalizes "3 + 0 = 3" and play continues. Player one on Team B places down a 4 and verbalizes "3 x 4 = 12" and play continues. Player one on Team A places down a 7 and verbalizes "12 - 7 = 5" and play continues. Player two on Team B lays down their Jack and verbalizes "11 + 5 = 16" and play continues.

Player two on Team A now lays down their Queen and verbalizes "16 - 12 = 4" and play continues. Player one on Team A plays their 2 and verbalizes "4 x 2 = 8" and play continues. Player one on Team B lays down a 1 and verbalizes "8 + 1 = 9". Player one collects all the cards (ie., 3, King, 4, 7, Jack, Queen, 2 and 1) and places them aside for points.

Teams continue to play until all the cards have been played or no other combinations can be made. A new target number is rolled for a new round of play. The team with the most cards (points) after three rounds wins.

COMBO FIVE

LEVEL: Grade 3 and up

SKILLS: Mixed operations (+, -, x, ÷), problem solving

PLAYERS: Teams of 2 vs. 2

EQUIPMENT: One 20-sided die, cards Ace - King (Ace = 1, Jack = 11, Queen = 12, King = 0)

GETTING STARTED: Both teams take five cards and place them face up. The goal of the game is to equal the rolled target number each round. To begin, one team rolls the target number for the round. This number will be used by both teams. Teams now begin finding combinations that equal the target number rolled - all operations may be used. A single card cannot be taken off. Teams may take off two, three, four or five card combinations. Teams may also take off a two card and a separate three card combination or two, two card combinations leaving one card behind for the next round. Each card may only be used once in any combination (ie., in the following example 4 can only be used once and not again in a second combination).

EXAMPLE: Cards drawn are as follows:

4	9	7	2	11
2	3	8	10	5

Target rolled = 11

Team One made the following combinations and removed the cards as follows:

9 + 2 = 11 and 4 + 7 = 11

leaving behind the **11** card as it was not used in any combination.

Team Two made the following combinations and removed the cards as follows:

(2 x 3) + 5 = 11

leaving behind the **8** and **10** cards.

Cards used in any combination are placed in the team's point pile and will be counted at the end of the game to determine the winner.

After each round both teams replenish their five cards. Team One in the above example will draw four new cards and Team Two will replenish theirs with three new ones as **8** and **10** were left behind.

A new target is rolled and players work with their new target and card combinations.

VARIATIONS:

To decrease the level of difficulty have players look for adding and subtracting combinations only.

Example: Cards drawn are as follows:

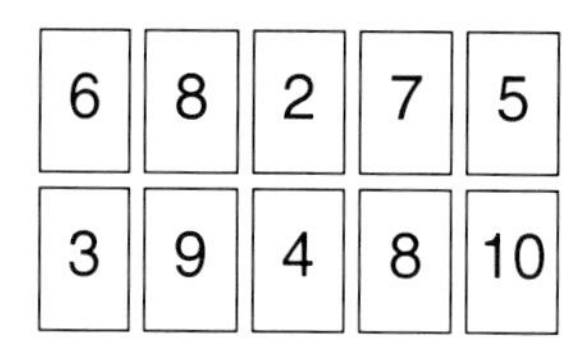

Target rolled = 6.

Team One made the following combinations and removed the cards as follows:

(7 + 5) - 6 = 6 and 8 - 2 = 6

Team One was successful in using all five cards in two separate combinations. Team One will be dealt five new cards for the next round.

Team Two made the following combinations and removed the cards as follows:

(8 + 10) - 9 - 3 = 6.

Team Two was left with their 4 card and the dealer will replenish with four new cards for the next round.

After a set period of time teams count their cards in their point piles. The team with the most points is the winner.

10 CARD PILE UP

LEVEL: Grade 4 and up

SKILLS: Mixed operations (+, -, x, ÷)

PLAYERS: 5, teams of 2 vs. 2 and 1 recorder

EQUIPMENT: One 20-sided die

GETTING STARTED: One player is selected to be the recorder who will record the math for the round. The other four players arrange themselves in teams of two, sitting opposite from each other. Each player is dealt six cards and holds them in such a manner that no one else can see them. A target number is rolled. The goal is for the players to reach this target number. All four operations can be used. The player to the right of the dealer begins the game. Player one lays down a card and verbalizes its value. The first card played cannot equal the target number rolled. Player two now selects any card from their hand and verbalizes any operation in combination with the previous example.

EXAMPLE: Target 15

Player one lays down a 3

Player two lays down a 5 and verbalizes 5 x 3 = 15. Player two takes the accumulated pile of cards (cards 3 and 5) and places them into their point pile.

Player three continues by starting back at 0. Players are still attempting to reach the target of 15. A new target number is rolled only when all cards or possible plays have been made.

EXAMPLE OF ROUND PLAYED OUT:

Player three lays down 10

Player four lays down 2, 10 + 2 = 12

Player one lays down 3 12 + 3 = 15

Player one takes the three card combination and places it into their point pile. The play goes back to 0.

Player two lays down 1

Player three lays down 8 1 x 8 = 8

Player four lays down 6 8 - 6 = 2

Player one lays down 9 2 x 9 = 18

Player two	lays down 10	18 - 10 = 8
Player three	lays down 0	8 + 0 = 8
Player four	lays down 9	8 + 9 = 17
Player one	lays down 2	17 - 2 = 15

Player one takes the eight card combination and places it into their point pile.

Player two	lays down 4	
Player three	lays down 6	4 x 6 = 24
Player four	lays down 8	24 ÷ 8 = 3
Player one	lays down 10	3 + 10 = 13
Player two	lays down 2	13 + 2 = 15

Player two takes the five card combination and places it into their point pile.

Player three	lays down 8	
Player four	lays down 1	8 x 1 = 8
Player one	lays down 1	8 - 1 = 7
Player two	lays down 9	7 + 9 = 16
Player three	lays down 7	16 - 7 = 9
Player four	lays down 4	9 + 4 = 13

Play ends

As no 15 combination was reached during the last round the cards are left discarded. A new round, with a new target number begins. Each player is dealt six new cards.

Play continues for a set period of time. The team with the most points wins.

Section V

NAME IT

LEVEL: Grade 2 and up

SKILLS: Identifying fractions, illustrating fractions

PLAYERS: 2

EQUIPMENT: One 12-sided die, pencil, paper

GETTING STARTED: Player one rolls the die and names that number in a fraction (ie., rolls a 6, names one-sixth). Player two must then draw a picture showing sixths.

EXAMPLE:

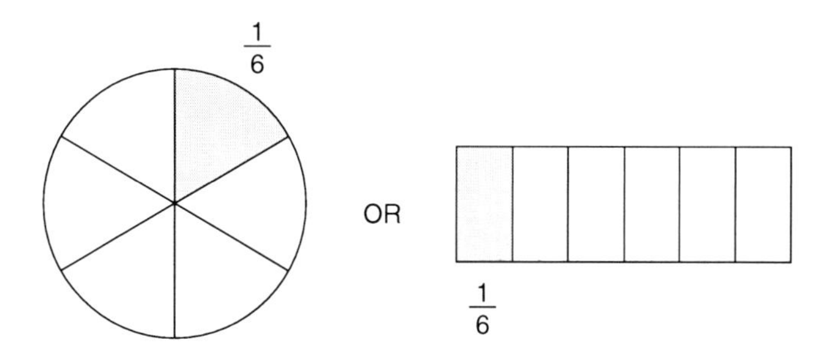

If the player correctly draws the corresponding fraction, they receive 1 point. Players alternate turns. The first player to score 10 points is the winner.

FUN FRACTIONS

LEVEL: Grade 3 and up

SKILLS: Identifying proper fractions, illustrating fractions

PLAYERS: 2

EQUIPMENT: Two 12-sided dice, pencil, paper

GETTING STARTED: Player one rolls the two dice and uses these two numbers to create a proper fraction (ie., rolls a 7 and a 12; seven-twelfths). Player then draws the fraction.

EXAMPLE:

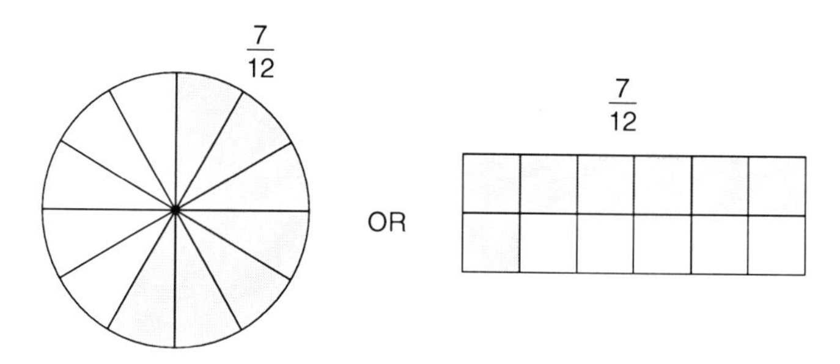

If the player draws the corresponding fraction correctly they receive 1 point. Players alternate turns. The first player to score 10 points is the winner.

FRACTION FRAZZLE

LEVEL: Grade 3 and up

SKILLS: Recognizing, naming and comparing fractions

PLAYERS: 2

EQUIPMENT: Two 12-sided dice, paper, pencil, and if possible fraction pieces to manipulate.

GETTING STARTED: Each player rolls two 12-sided dice and records their fraction as a proper fraction. Example, player one rolls a 3 and 7, verbalizes "three-sevenths", records 3/7 and builds this fraction with manipulatives or draws this fraction, ie.,

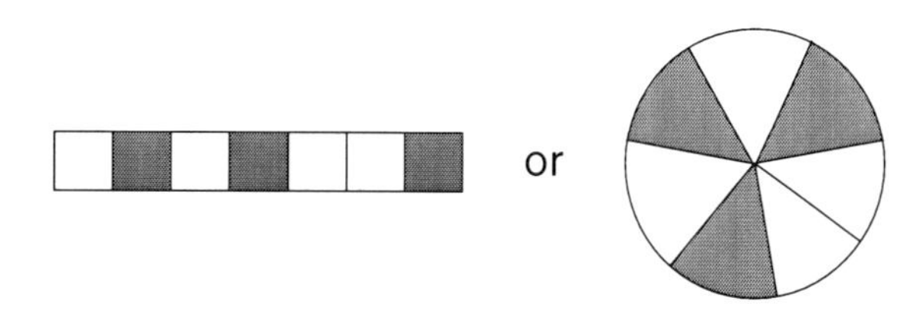

Player two rolls a 5 and 10 and verbalizes "five-tenths" and records 5/10 and draws this fraction or builds it with manipulatives.

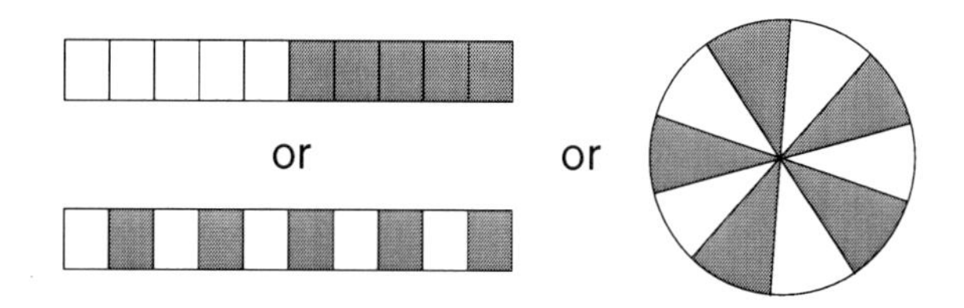

Players must now compare their fractions and the player with the greatest fraction (closer to one whole) earns 1 point.

If players tie, (ie., their fractions are equal in comparison) then both players earn 1 point.

FRACE

LEVEL: Grade 3 and up

SKILLS: Identifying and naming fractions

PLAYERS: 2 (equal skill level)

EQUIPMENT: Two 12-sided dice, one per player

GETTING STARTED: At the same time each player rolls one die. The first player to give the proper fraction name earns 1 point. In the event of a tie (ie., both players say their answer at the same time), no point is earned. The first player to score 20 points is the winner.

EXAMPLE: Rolls = 5 and 9

Player one verbalizes "five-ninths" before player two, and thus player one earns 1 point.

Rolls = 2 and 8

Player two verbalizes "two-eighths" before player one, and thus player two earns 1 point.

VARIATION: To increase difficulty the players verbalize the fraction in its simplest-reduced form.

ie., Roll = 4 and 12

Players would verbalize "one-third" (1/3).

ie., Roll = 2 and 6

Players would verbalize "one-third" (1/3).

FRIENDLY FRACTIONS

LEVEL:	Grade 4 and up
SKILLS:	Comparing fractions
PLAYERS:	2
EQUIPMENT:	Two 12-sided dice, paper, pencil
GETTING STARTED:	Each player rolls the two dice and creates the largest fraction possible. Players verbalize and record their fractions. Players compare their fractions and the player with the greatest fraction earns 1 point.
EXAMPLE:	Player one: Roll = 7 and 9: 9/7 = 1 2/7. Player one verbalizes "one and two-sevenths".

Player two: Roll = 6 and 3: 6/3 = 2. Player two verbalizes "two-wholes" or "two".

Player two earns 1 point and now verbalizes "two-wholes are greater than one and two-sevenths".

In the event of a tie, players roll new fractions, re-compare and the player with the greatest fraction for that round earns 2 points.

FRACTION DOUBLES

LEVEL: Grade 4 and up

SKILLS: Doubles, comparing fractions, simplifying fractions, finding common denominators

PLAYERS: 2

EQUIPMENT: Two 12-sided dice, paper, pencil

GETTING STARTED: Each player rolls one 12-sided die and names their fraction in its simplest form. Each player must then double their fraction and say the name of their new fraction outloud. The player with the greatest fraction earns 1 point.

EXAMPLE: Player one rolls a 4 and says “1/4 and its double is 2/8”.

Player two rolls a 9 and says “1/9 and its double is 2/18”.

Player one then verbalizes the math equation “2/8 is greater than 2/18” and player one earns 1 point.

VARIATION I: Each player rolls two 12-sided dice and creates a proper fraction and then doubles it (ie., player one rolls a 5 and 8 and verbalizes “5/8 and its double is 10/16”. Player two rolls a 2 and 7 and verbalizes “2/7 and its double is 4/14”. Player one would now verbalize “10/16 is greater than 4/14” and player one would earn 1 point).

VARIATION II: Play a snap-speed variation where at the same time each player rolls one 12-sided die and players silently name the proper fraction. Each player must then double this fraction and say its name outloud.

EXAMPLE: Player one’s roll = 8
Player two’s roll = 2
2/8 doubled = 4/16

Whichever player verbalizes “4/16” first would earn 1 point. If players tie, ie., both verbalize the answer at the same time, then both players would earn 1 point.

VARIATION III: Each player rolls one die at the same time. The goal of the game is to be the first player to reduce the fraction rolled to its simplest form (silently) and then double it and name this new fraction outloud. The first player to do so would earn 1 point.

EXAMPLE:

Player one 12 }
Player two 4 } 4/12 reduced

1/3 doubled = 2/6.

FRACTION FREEZE

LEVEL: Grade 4 and up

SKILLS: Adding fractions

PLAYERS: 2

EQUIPMENT: Two 12-sided dice, paper, pencil, fraction pieces (optional)

GETTING STARTED: The goal of the game is to create the fraction closest to one-whole, after three possible turns. Player one begins by rolling both dice, naming and recording their fraction in proper form and deciding whether to freeze or roll again on a future turn.

Player two now rolls and does the same. If one player chooses to freeze they do not roll again and the other player may continue on for a possible additional two rolls (their fractions are added together as rolls accumulate). Once all rolls have been taken or both players have chosen to freeze, both players compare their fractions or sum of fractions to one another. The player with the fraction closest to one-whole without going over earns 1 point for the round. If any or both players create a fraction of EXACTLY one-whole, then 2 points are earned.

EXAMPLE: **<u>Player One</u>:** Roll = 6 and 11 6/11 "six-elevenths". Player one chooses not to freeze and will take an additional turn.

<u>Player Two:</u> Roll = 1 and 5 1/5 "one-fifth". Player two chooses not to freeze and will take an additional turn.

<u>Player One</u>: Roll = 2 and 11 2/11 "two-elevenths". Player one adds their two fractions together and verbalizes their sum. 6/11 + 2/11 = 8/11 and player one chooses to freeze.

<u>Player Two:</u> Roll = 4 and 10 4/10 "four-tenths". Player two adds 1/5 + 4/10 = 6/10 and chooses to roll one more time. Player two takes their third and final turn and rolls one and two and verbalizes "one-half". Player two adds 6/10 + 1/2 = 6/10 + 5/10 = 11/10 or 1 1/10. Player two's fraction is greater than one whole. Player one earns 1 point for the round for being closest to one whole without going over.

VARIATION:

Players can choose to record their rolls but not verbalize. Player may choose to secretly roll their fractions, record them and play as previously directed. A third player is involved as the judge for each round and players compare their fractions at the end of the play for comparison. The player with the fraction closest to one-whole is the winner.

HIDE AND SEEK

LEVEL: Grade 3 and up

SKILLS: Graphing, identifying coordinates

PLAYERS: 2

EQUIPMENT: Two 12-sided dice per player, one grid per player (see reproducibles), pencil

GETTING STARTED: Each player has a gameboard and hides ten points (●) on their grid. Player one rolls the dice and calls them out as coordinates (player chooses which way to call them, (ie., either [2,3] or [3,2]). Player two checks their grid and calls "found" or "seek". Player one records the find or seek on their own grid. If it is a "found", player one takes another turn. Players alternate turns until one player finds all of the other player's hidden points.

EXAMPLE:

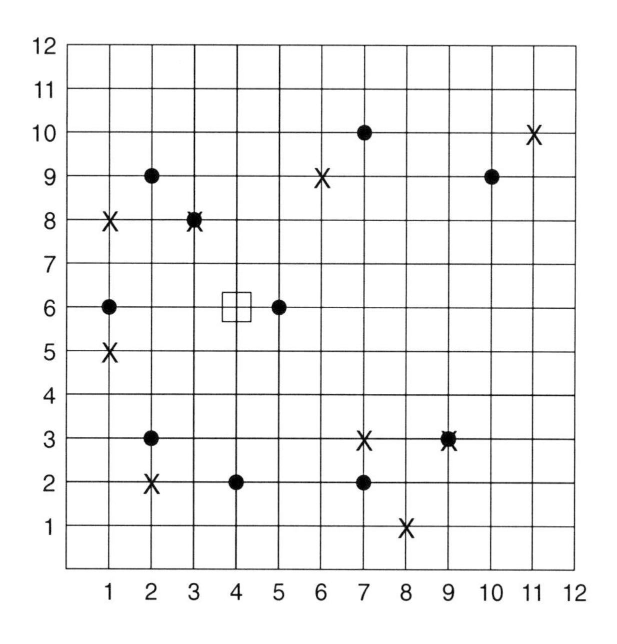

TARGET THREE

LEVEL: Grade 3 and up

SKILLS: Graphing

PLAYERS: 2

EQUIPMENT: Two 10-sided dice per player, gameboard (see reproducibles), pencil

GETTING STARTED: Players use one gameboard. One player is 'X', the other is '●'. The goal of the game is to get three coordinates in a row; either horizontally, vertically or diagonally. Player 'X' rolls the dice, identifies the coordinates, locates it on the grid and marks it by placing an 'X' (player chooses what order to call the rolls, (ie., either [2,5] or [5,2]). Player '●' then rolls the dice, identifies the coordinates, locates the appropriate place on the grid, and marks the spot with an '●'. Players alternate turns. If a player lands on a point with their own mark, the player takes another turn. If a player lands on a point occupied by another player, they score a point, circle the mark, and it is now out of play (ie., 6,2).

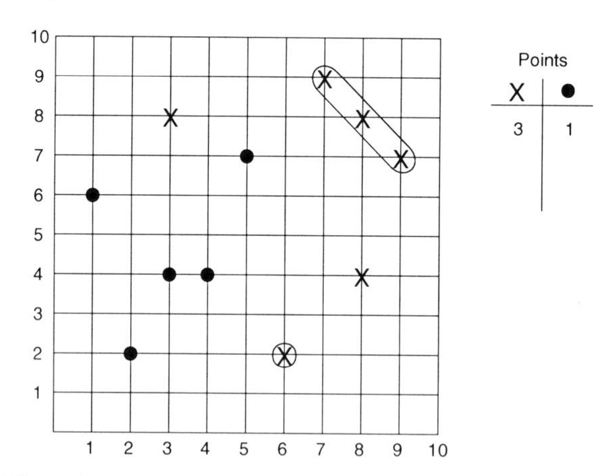

EXAMPLE: The player rolls 9 and 7, so coordinates can be either (9,7) or (7,9).

The player decides which would be more advantageous to their play and marks their grid accordingly.

When a player gets three coordinates in a row they are circled. They would then score three points. Play continues for a set period of time. The player with the most points is the winner.

Reproducibles

ROLLING ALONG

1 2 3 4 5 6 7 8 9 10 11 12
X X X

1 2 3 4 5 6 7 8 9 10 11 12
X X X

1 2 3 4 5 6 7 8 9 10 11 12
X X X

1 2 3 4 5 6 7 8 9 10 11 12
X X X

1 2 3 4 5 6 7 8 9 10 11 12
X X X

1 2 3 4 5 6 7 8 9 10 11 12
X X X

1 2 3 4 5 6 7 8 9 10 11 12
X X X

NUMBO

STANDARD				
1	2	3	4	5
6	7	8	9	10
11	12	13	14	15
16	17	18	19	20

RANDOM				
5	1	14	10	4
16	6	19	7	2
17	3	8	18	12
9	13	11	15	20

ROLL IT AND MARK IT

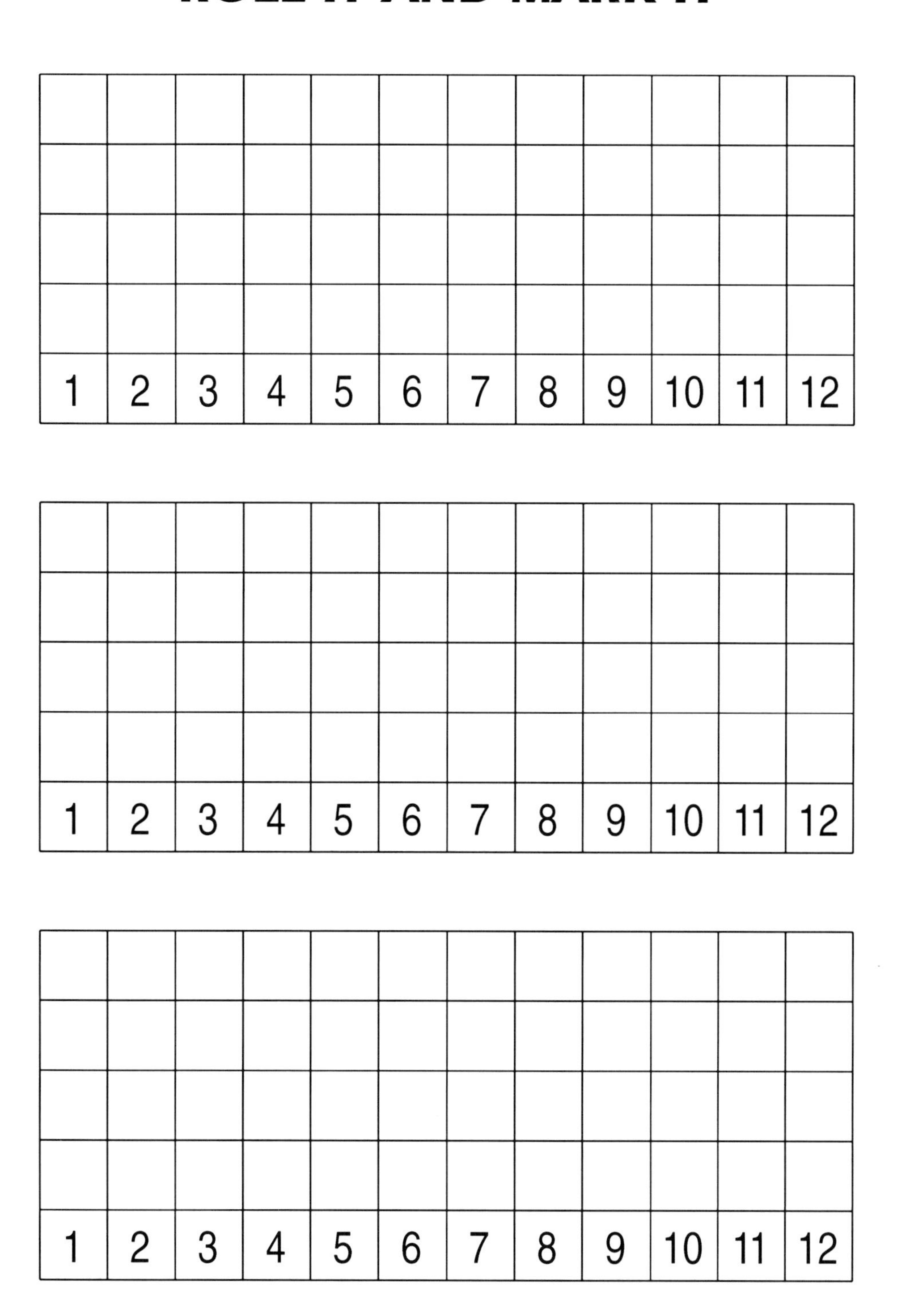

RACE TO THE TOP

10		
9		
8		
7		
6		
5		
4		
3		
2		
1		
	ODD	EVEN

TIME OUT

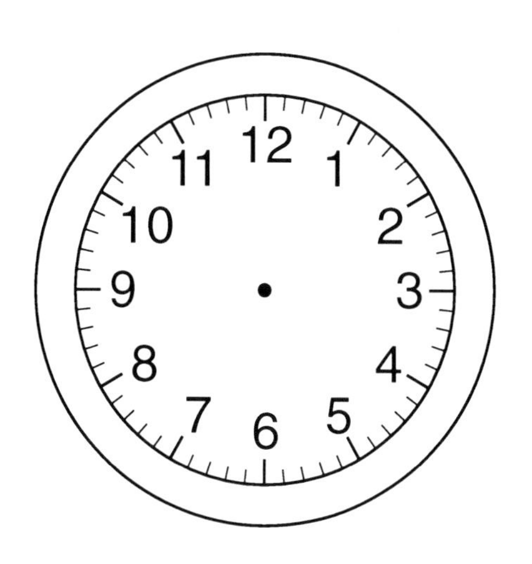
12
1
2
3
4
5
6
7
8
9
10
11

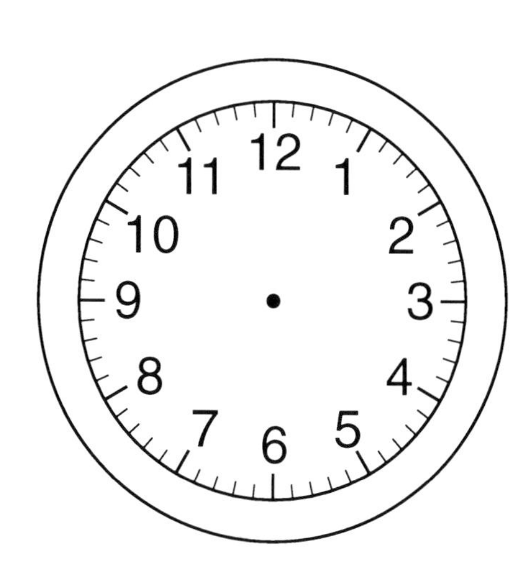
12
1
2
3
4
5
6
7
8
9
10
11

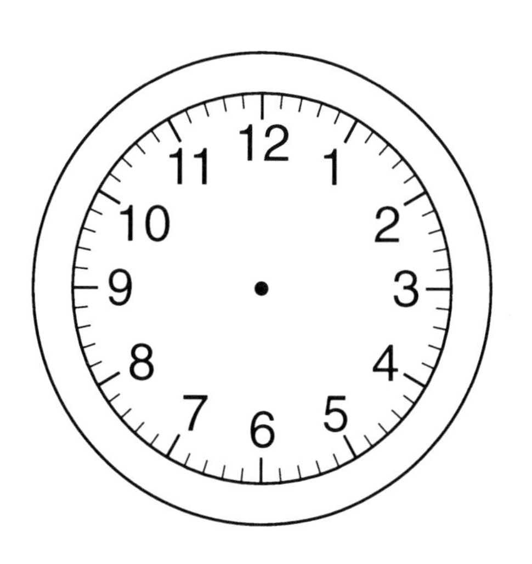
12
1
2
3
4
5
6
7
8
9
10
11

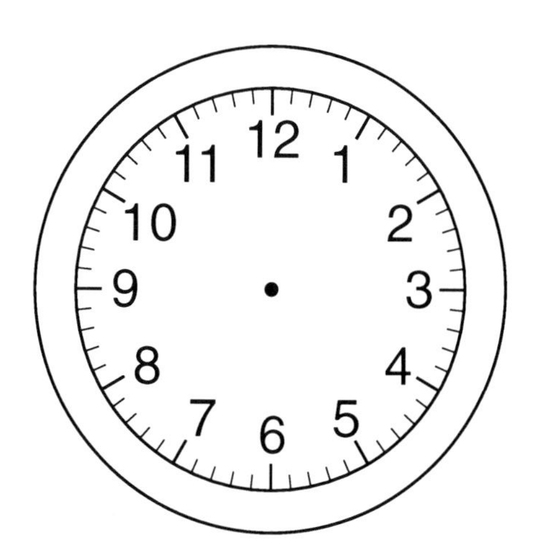
12
1
2
3
4
5
6
7
8
9
10
11

HUNDRED BOARD

1	2	3	4	5	6	7	8	9	10
11	12	13	14	15	16	17	18	19	20
21	22	23	24	25	26	27	28	29	30
31	32	33	34	35	36	37	38	39	40
41	42	43	44	45	46	47	48	49	50
51	52	53	54	55	56	57	58	59	60
61	62	63	64	65	66	67	68	69	70
71	72	73	74	75	76	77	78	79	80
81	82	83	84	85	86	87	88	89	90
91	92	93	94	95	96	97	98	99	100

WINNING TRACK CHALLENGER

0 1 2 3 4 5 6 7 8 9 10 11 12
X X X

0 1 2 3 4 5 6 7 8 9 10 11 12
X X X

0 1 2 3 4 5 6 7 8 9 10 11 12
X X X

0 1 2 3 4 5 6 7 8 9 10 11 12
X X X

0 1 2 3 4 5 6 7 8 9 10 11 12
X X X

0 1 2 3 4 5 6 7 8 9 10 11 12
X X X

0 1 2 3 4 5 6 7 8 9 10 11 12
X X X

ADDITION TIC TAC TOE

	0	1	2	3	4	5	6	7	8	9
0	0	1	2	3	4	5	6	7	8	9
1	1	2	3	4	5	6	7	8	9	10
2	2	3	4	5	6	7	8	9	10	11
3	3	4	5	6	7	8	9	10	11	12
4	4	5	6	7	8	9	10	11	12	13
5	5	6	7	8	9	10	11	12	13	14
6	6	7	8	9	10	11	12	13	14	15
7	7	8	9	10	11	12	13	14	15	16
8	8	9	10	11	12	13	14	15	16	17
9	9	10	11	12	13	14	15	16	17	18

FILL 'ER UP

1 2 3 4 5 6 7 8 9 10 11 12 13 14 15 16 17 18 19 20 21 22 23 24 25 26 27 28 29 30

SQUARE DOUBLING

4.↓ 2.↓

1.→

3.→

4.↓ 2.↓

1.→

3.→

YOUR BOARD OR MINE?

1	2	3	4	5
6	7	8	9	10
11	12	13	14	15
16	17	18	19	20

1	2	3	4	5
6	7	8	9	10
11	12	13	14	15
16	17	18	19	20

SUBTRACT-A-GRAPH

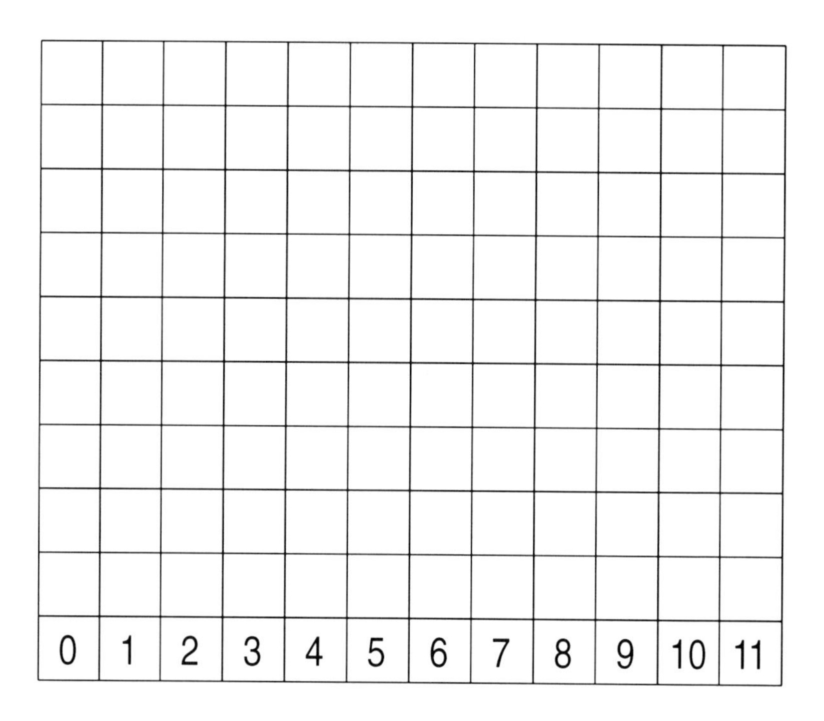

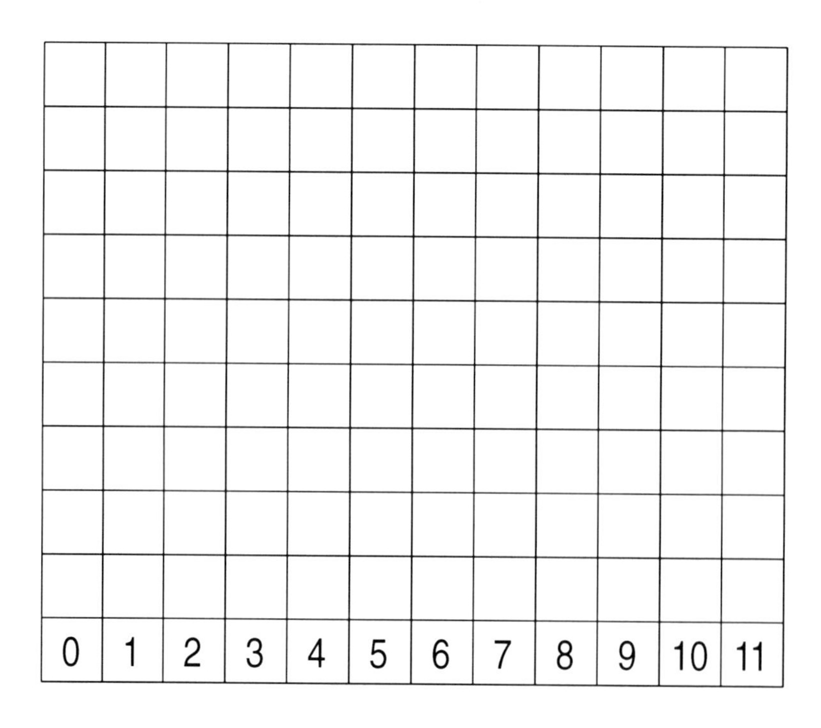

SUB TRACK

0 1 2 3 4 5 6 7 8 9 10 11
X X X

0 1 2 3 4 5 6 7 8 9 10 11
X X X

0 1 2 3 4 5 6 7 8 9 10 11
X X X

0 1 2 3 4 5 6 7 8 9 10 11
X X X

0 1 2 3 4 5 6 7 8 9 10 11
X X X

0 1 2 3 4 5 6 7 8 9 10 11
X X X

0 1 2 3 4 5 6 7 8 9 10 11
X X X

REACH FOR THE TOP

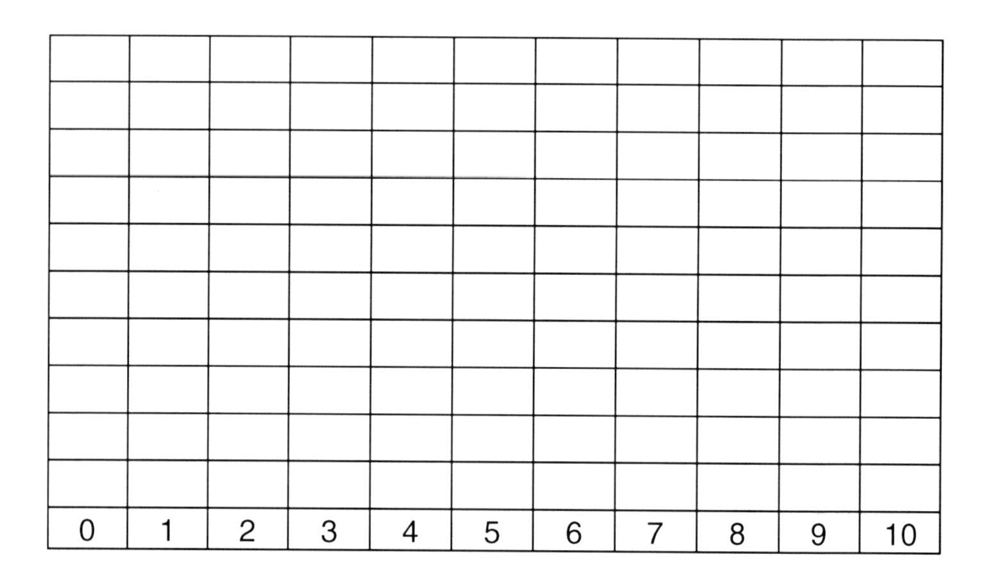

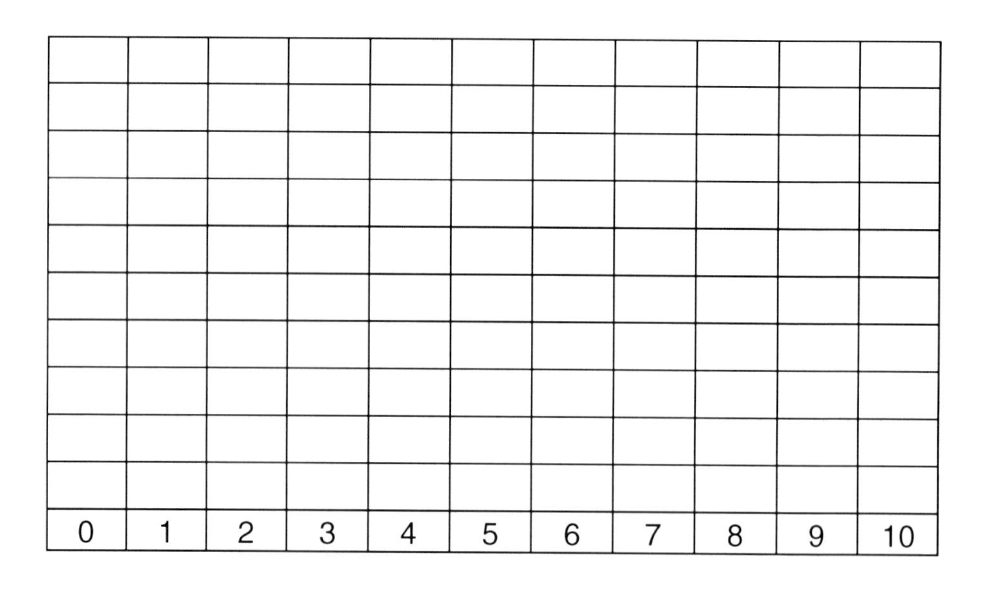

CROSS OVERS

MULTIPLICATION SCRAMBLE

0 - 9	________
10 - 19	________
20 - 29	________
30 - 39	________
40 - 49	________
50 - 59	________
60 - 69	________
70 - 79	________
80 - 89	________
90 - 99	________
100 - 109	________
110 - 119	________
120 - 129	________
130 - 139	________
140 - 149	________

0 - 9	________
10 - 19	________
20 - 29	________
30 - 39	________
40 - 49	________
50 - 59	________
60 - 69	________
70 - 79	________
80 - 89	________
90 - 99	________
100 - 109	________
110 - 119	________
120 - 129	________
130 - 139	________
140 - 149	________

0 - 9	________
10 - 19	________
20 - 29	________
30 - 39	________
40 - 49	________
50 - 59	________
60 - 69	________
70 - 79	________
80 - 89	________
90 - 99	________
100 - 109	________
110 - 119	________
120 - 129	________
130 - 139	________
140 - 149	________

0 - 9	________
10 - 19	________
20 - 29	________
30 - 39	________
40 - 49	________
50 - 59	________
60 - 69	________
70 - 79	________
80 - 89	________
90 - 99	________
100 - 109	________
110 - 119	________
120 - 129	________
130 - 139	________
140 - 149	________

THE BIG ROUND UP

10 20 30 40 50 60 70 80 90 100 110 120 130 140

10 20 30 40 50 60 70 80 90 100 110 120 130 140

10 20 30 40 50 60 70 80 90 100 110 120 130 140

10 20 30 40 50 60 70 80 90 100 110 120 130 140

10 20 30 40 50 60 70 80 90 100 110 120 130 140

10 20 30 40 50 60 70 80 90 100 110 120 130 140

10 20 30 40 50 60 70 80 90 100 110 120 130 140

10 20 30 40 50 60 70 80 90 100 110 120 130 140

10 20 30 40 50 60 70 80 90 100 110 120 130 140

10 20 30 40 50 60 70 80 90 100 110 120 130 140

ON TARGET

					TARGET NUMBER					
	x		=		10		=		x	
	x		=		20		=		x	
	x		=		30		=		x	
	x		=		40		=		x	
	x		=		50		=		x	
	x		=		60		=		x	
	x		=		70		=		x	
	x		=		80		=		x	
	x		=		90		=		x	
	x		=		100		=		x	

THREE FOR ME

	1	2	3	4	5	6	7	8	9	10	11	12
1	1	2	3	4	5	6	7	8	9	10	11	12
2	2	4	6	8	10	12	14	16	18	20	22	24
3	3	6	9	12	15	18	21	24	27	30	33	36
4	4	8	12	16	20	24	28	32	36	40	44	48
5	5	10	15	20	25	30	35	40	45	50	55	60
6	6	12	18	24	30	36	42	48	54	60	66	72
7	7	14	21	28	35	42	49	56	63	70	77	84
8	8	16	24	32	40	48	56	64	72	80	88	96
9	9	18	27	36	45	54	63	72	81	90	99	108
10	10	20	30	40	50	60	70	80	90	100	110	120
11	11	22	33	44	55	66	77	88	99	110	121	132
12	12	24	36	48	60	72	84	96	108	120	132	144

SPEEDY GRAPHING

0 1 2 3 4 5 6 7 8 9 10 11 12 13 14 15 16 17 18

0 1 2 3 4 5 6 7 8 9 10 11 12 13 14 15 16 17 18

TANGLE WITH TWENTY

0 1 2 3 4 5 6 7 8 9 10 11 12 13 14 15 16 17 18 19 20

X X X

0 1 2 3 4 5 6 7 8 9 10 11 12 13 14 15 16 17 18 19 20

X X X

0 1 2 3 4 5 6 7 8 9 10 11 12 13 14 15 16 17 18 19 20

X X X

0 1 2 3 4 5 6 7 8 9 10 11 12 13 14 15 16 17 18 19 20

X X X

0 1 2 3 4 5 6 7 8 9 10 11 12 13 14 15 16 17 18 19 20

X X X

0 1 2 3 4 5 6 7 8 9 10 11 12 13 14 15 16 17 18 19 20

X X X

0 1 2 3 4 5 6 7 8 9 10 11 12 13 14 15 16 17 18 19 20

X X X

HIDE AND SEEK

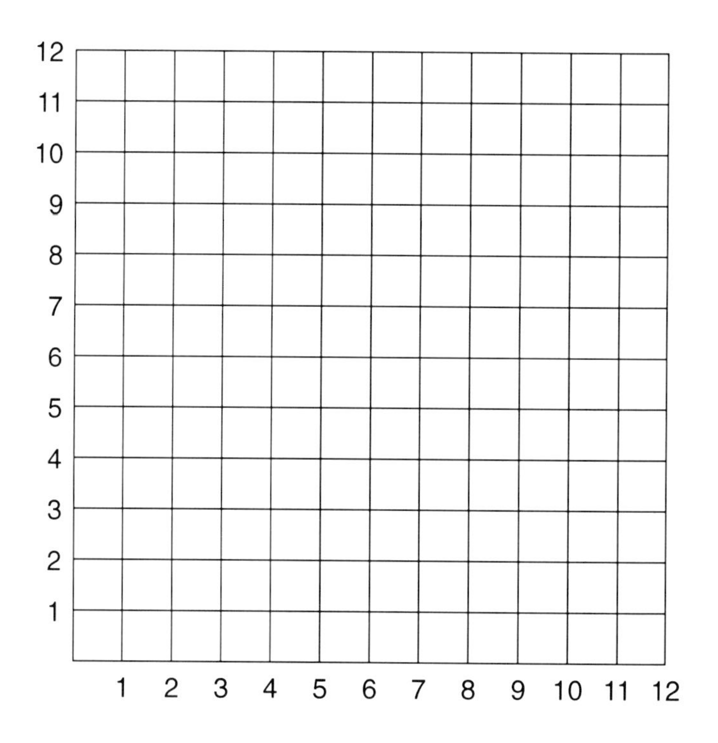

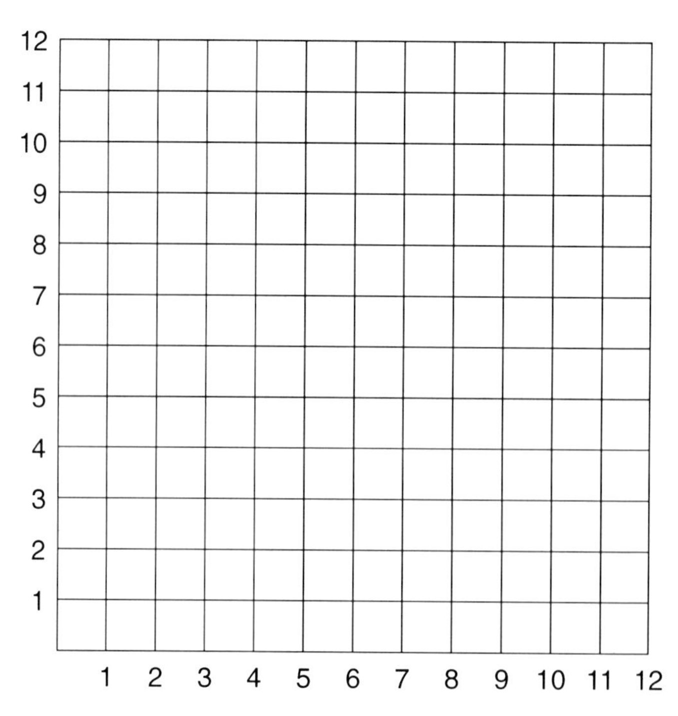

TARGET THREE

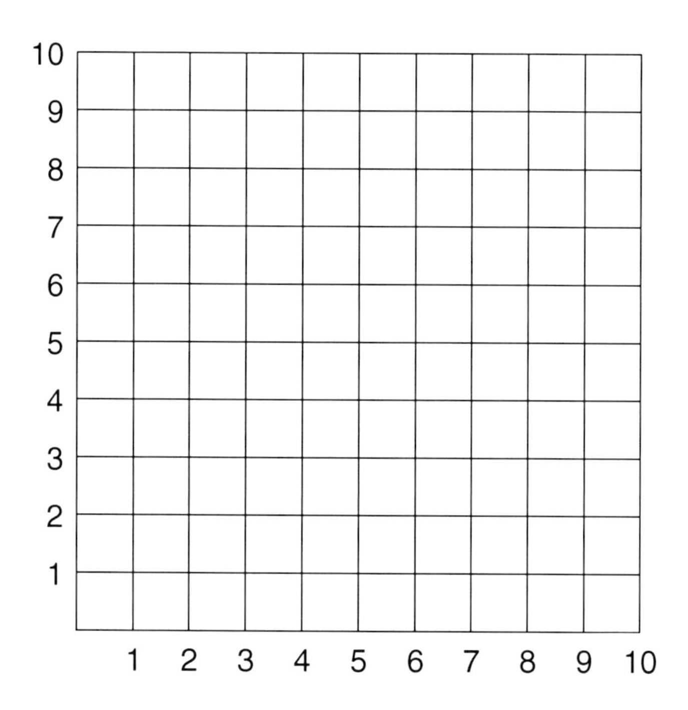

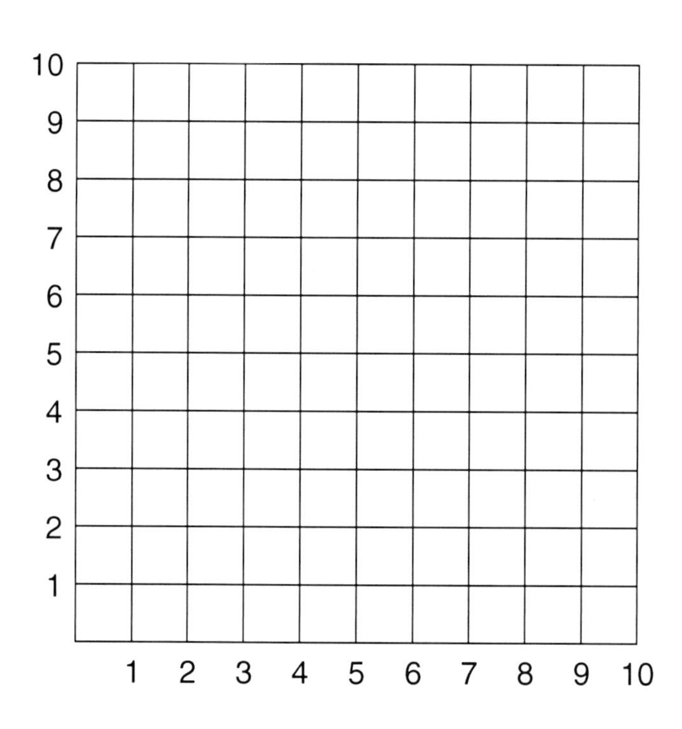

Appendix of Skills

box cars and one-eyed jacks®

About the Authors

The BOX CARS & ONE-EYED JACKS team of Joanne Currah and Jane Felling bring both innovation and inspiration to their consulting. They have combined expertise in elementary and special education and have conducted extensive research into the area of Games as a Teaching Strategy.

The authors developed all of the games for BOX CARS AND ONE-EYED JACKS Volume I "Shuffling Into Math" while teaching in their classrooms. Since the original publication in 1989, the authors have been successfully inservicing across Canada, the United States, Europe, Australia and Asia.

In 1991 BOX CARS won a National Award from the Learning Disabilities Association.

During 1992 BOX CARS Volume II "All Hands on Deck" and Volume III "Dice Works" were published to meet the growing demand by teachers and parents for new material. Their math books and manipulatives were intended for Kindergarten to Grade 7 and incorporated the use of cards, dice, and special ten, twelve, twenty, and thirty-sided dice. In 1994 "Money Matters for Kids" (Canadian Version) and "Rolling In The Dough" (American Version) Volumes IV and Volume V "Math Attack with 30-Sided Dice" were published. Volumes I, II, and III reached National Best Selling status in 1994!!

"On a Roll to Spelling", published in 1995 led the authors in a brand new direction with their games. Eagerly awaited by both teachers and parents, "On a Roll to Spelling" quickly became a favourite! This volume incorporated the use of alphabet dice and letter tiles and was designed to put the fun back into Spelling! Stratedice came next. Stratedice is a unique tray of 36 dice and gamebook. It also was published in 1995 and has reached Best Selling status.

"Piece it Together with Fractions" was completed in 1997. This games book comes with special fraction dice and manipulatives that make fractions fun and easy to understand. A new tactile spelling games book, "Spelling Rules... With These Cool Tools!" came next and was a great addition to the language games. Decadice was completed in 2000. This games book is an author favourite as it includes numerous "Thought Provokers" to challenge game players of all ages.

The authors marked 2001 with the publication of Radical Math - Millennium Edition. It was a most challenging and rewarding project for them both!

After a break, Jane and Joanne published two specialty books "Double Dare You" using unique double dice and "Power Play - Games for Place Value". Both continue to workshop and bring their passion for games as a teaching strategy to thousands of teachers across North America.

What's Your Game Plan For Staff Development?

BASIC MATH GAMES WORKSHOP *

LEVELS: K-3, 4-6, 7-9, Special Education

Participants will play a selection of math games from the award winning Box Cars & One Eyed Jacks series. The workshop will focus on basic card and regular dice games and will cover ideas for teaching numeration, mental math, all operations, place value, graphing, data gathering, cooperative games, integers and more. Strategies are provided throughout. Problem solving is integrated into the games and can be adapted to suit the needs of all students to complement any existing math program. Ideas for resource and classroom management will be provided as well as great ideas for math journals. Get back to the basics.

SHUFFLING INTO MATH PRIMARY MATH GAMES

LEVELS: K-3

Come prepared to play a selection of primary math games using a variety of dice and playing cards. Areas covered will include place value, number sense, operations, graphing, probability and more. Ideas for cooperative games, homework support, student samples and more will be shared. Be ready to shake, rattle and roll.

Call
1-866-DICE FUN
to Book Your
Workshop

OPERATION BOX CARS

LEVELS: K-3, 4-9 or 1-6

This strategy based workshop focuses on the best card, dice and multi-sided dice games that help learners understand and master addition, subtraction, multiplication and division. By connecting strategies with game's practice students will become more empowered and successful. This workshop is for you if you want to help your students develop understanding, proficiency and confidence when it comes time to "operate".

PROBABILITY FUN 'DIE' MENTALS

LEVELS: K-3, 4-6, 7-9

The best Box Cars games that put the "eye popping" back into probability. The games will help your students discover the "wow ...that's amazing" of this part of the curriculum. Game activities will extend and connect the learning for students into data management, graphing, outcomes, beginning statistics, predicting and more. Come prepared to Shake Rattle and Roll with all kinds of dice that put the fun back into probability.

POWER PLAY - GAMES FOR PLACE VALUE

LEVELS: 1-3, 4-9 or 1-6

Get your students on the "power play team". Our most kid popular games that will empower your students with all kinds of strategies, mental math techniques, tricks, tips and more. Games will cover place value, rounding, decimals, and more, and will incorporate the use of cards, dice and multi-sided dice. Come prepared to train your brain on games!

Visit our website for more information at
www.boxcarsandoneeyedjacks.com

DOUBLE DARE YOU
LEVELS: K-3, 4-7
This strategy based workshop focuses on the newest dice to hit the math manipulative world. DOUBLE DICE are highly motivating to students and have a wide range of mathematical uses. Come prepared to play games that cover the following areas: operations, fractions, place value and probability. Unique double regular dice, double 10 and 12-sided dice, and three-in-a-cube dice will be used. We double dare you to add some fun into your math program. Come prepared to play.

BOX CARS RADICAL MATH *
Middle Years: 5-9 or 7-9, Special Education
An interactive games workshop using cards, dice and multi-sided dice with a "back to basics" approach. By combining games and problem solving teachers are able to maintain high interest even from the low level student. Areas covered include integers, place value, decimals, operations, order of operation, probability, problem solving, data management and more!

LITERACY FUN "DIE" MENTALS - LITERACY GAMES
LEVELS: K-3, 4-6 or K-6, 7-9, Plus Special Needs
Are you a Teacher who is seeking multi-sensory, integrated language activities for your students? This is a hands-on workshop that integrates spelling and reading/literacy skills through the use of cooperative learning games. Unique alphabet dice, stackable letter tiles and decks of sight word cards are some of the motivating materials used to enhance literacy development. Handouts will include reproducible gameboards. Many practical take-home ideas for your students will be shared. Come prepared to get "On A Roll" with Box Cars.

BOX CARS SCHOOL VISITS / MODEL LESSONS *
LEVELS: Elementary - Junior High (Middle Years)
Consultants visit a school for a day and teach as many students as possible. Teachers watch, play and learn strategies right along with their "real students" and experience how it works. Strategies for classroom management and organization are brought to life for teachers who can immediately follow up the visit with implementation. Parents can be invited and participate right along with their children. The entire school community benefits. This workshop is often combined with a Family Math Night.

FAMILY MATH NIGHTS OR PARENT WORKSHOPS *
LEVELS: K-3, 4-6, 7-9
Have parents and students come and play a wide variety of math games that use cards and dice from the award winning Box Cars & One-Eyed Jacks series. During the workshop families will play a wide variety of games to review and strengthen math concepts. Great ideas and strategies will be taught to help students learn the basics. Games are a fun way to provide homework support to your parents and build success and self-esteem for your students. Get your community "shake, rattle and rolling" with this excellent workshop.

* Most suitable for Title I programs

box cars and one-eyed jacks®

Box Cars and One-Eyed Jacks Series Includes:

Shuffling Into Math - Kindergarten to Grade 3

All Hands on Deck - Grade 1 to 9

Dice Works - Kindergarten to Grade 9

Rolling In The Dough - Kindergarten to Grade 9

Math Attack - Kindergarten to Grade 9

On a Roll to Spelling and More - Kindergarten to Grade 7

Piece it Together with Fractions - Grade 1 to 9

Deca Dice - Grade 1 to 9

Radical Math - Grade 6 to 12

Stratedice Dice Games - Kindergarten to Grade 7

Power Play Games For Place Value - Grade 1 to 9

Double Dare You - Double Dice Games - Grade 1 to 9

Spelling Rules With These Cool Tools - Kindergarten to Grade